Wake Up To Human Life

Imam W. Deen Mohammed®

ISBN-13: 978-1470022419

CONTENTS

Imam W. Deen Mohammed, *leader of the largest community of Muslims in the United States of America passed on September 9, 2008. We pray that his work continues to grow and serve humanity as he would have desired it to, through all of us who have benefited so greatly from his teachings.*

Ameen

Structure, Guard And Publish The Knowledge

"We need knowledge, then we need protection for it. How do you protect knowledge? Some people say, "You protect knowledge by not letting anybody interfere with it. Don't let anybody change it. Publish it! When you publish it, people know it. That's its protection." Yes! If you want to protect your knowledge, publish it! When you publish it, it is protected and the people know it. But if you keep it locked up to yourself, you will die and your knowledge will die with you. Or your enemy will get a hold to it and he will publish it after you in a corrupt form.

Thus, Allah (swt) says. "And We have revealed it for the express purpose that it should be propagated." Yes! That is its guarantee that it will be protected. When it's propagated in its right form, then the people will inherit it directly. They don't have to listen to what you have to say. You won't have to tell them what Prophet Muhammad (pbuh) said, they got it directly. It was published by him in his lifetime.

If we want to guard the knowledge that we have, we must publish it. The more people know about it, the more it is guaranteed that it will live and it won't be changed. The less people know about it, the better the chance that it will die with us, or be changed. Yes! We structure the knowledge and we propagate the knowledge." *Imam W. Deen Mohammed*

Abbreviations Clarified

G-d for God
In this book the word God is written as G-d for the respect of the word "god" because some people mirror to disrespect it with the word "dog".

SWT for Subhana Wa Tallah
The abbreviation after Allah (SWT) means "Subhana Wa Tallah" in Arabic which means "The Sacred and The Mighty" in English.

PBUH for Peace Be Upon Him
The abbreviation after Prophet Muhammad (PBUH) means "May the Peace and Blessings of Allah (G-d) be upon him" in English and "Sal Allahu Allahi Wa Salam" in Arabic.

AS for Alayhi Salam
The abbreviation (AS) means "Alayhi Salam" in Arabic, which means "May Allah (G-d) bless him" in English.

CHAPTER 1

BETTER SITUATE OURSELVES INSIDE OF OUR OWN SOCIETY

**Markham, IL
September 8, 2002**

Peace be unto you, As-Salaam-Alaikum. It means the same. We thank Allah (swt), G-d, for our life and all that supports our life. We thank Him for this day we have here, a day of pleasure and a day of serious thought. We worship G-d and we thank G-d for His Servants, the Messengers, the Prophets.

We salute the last of the Prophets, Muhammad (pbuh), with the salutation, the Prayers and the Peace of G-d be upon him, and upon His Servants, the righteous, all, ameen.
See how close we are to the Christians? We say "ameen" and they say "amen.-" Although today I am here to talk about something we have a need for, a spirit for.

Any human being has a spirit for what I will share here today. My spirit for it was so strong that it shaped my speech in the Nation of Islam and it has shaped my speech since I was a Minister in the Nation of Islam.
A senior member of the Nation of Islam sent me this tape, and it was a tape of Malcolm X introducing me, around 1957 or 1958. He had invited me to speak, and it was not in New York. Malcolm was responsible for many cities outside of New York and away from the East Coast.

I spoke briefly and set down, and Malcolm whispered to me: "Minister Wallace, they want to hear more." So I got up and continued where I left off or had concluded before. I did have more to say, so I continued.

I listened to that tape the senior member sent to me and said, "I am surprised. What I said then is what I am saying now! There is no difference." Although I didn't have the formal opening that I have now, I did use the opening we used back then when we would say: "We thank Allah (swt) for the Honorable Elijah Muhammad."

We Need To Be More In Charge Of Our Lives, Period

What I was talking about then is what I am going to talk about now. We need to be more in charge of our lives, period. But that doesn't go for just us African Americans or Blacks, it goes for all people nowadays. The world has changed so, that you have to spend too much time to have serious thought about your own lives.

Even when someone says, "how are you," we are not thinking about it. The only time we really think about this is

when we get a five-day notice or the house catches on fire or
the dope fiend's son does something to get us upset.

We only think of our life when some great tragedy occurs. At
other times, we are so busy working and trying to pay the
bills. Or we are busy being entertained by Satan, and he can
keep all of us busy. I am talking about that time you are
giving to what you know to be wrong.

We spoke of the "great seers" before we called them
prophets. Don't you know the great seers saw this coming?
They said a time is coming when man, the individual person,
will be so occupied with his own concerns, that he won't
have time for anybody else. Isn't that the world now?
The mother is so busy, she doesn't have the time that she
would like to give to her children. Individuals in the family
are so busy, they can't give time to the family. They are all
going their separate ways, in their separate worlds doing their
separate things. So the times that these great minds and
visionaries and psychic people, those G-d blessed with
special psychic powers. That time is right here now.

They told us the city was going to become bigger and bigger
and that the population was going to become more and more.

That the cities would become the main places for sin and corruption. That has happened already. It would be so bad, the righteous were going to find no comfort anywhere. There was going to be no peace for the righteous, except in their own souls.

If you are a good person, no matter how much bad is around you, you can be right in the midst of hell and your goodness will be your protection. You will think about the misery all around you, and it will make you sad. But it does not take away your peace.

Even if it is your special daughter, the one you admired the most, goes and get involved in drugs and prostitution and becomes such a sad thing in your life, you might even say: "Sometimes I wish I were dead. I would rather be dead, than to see her like this." But that is only when you are thinking about her. Otherwise, she does not take away your peace.

You have something in the center of your life, centered inside, that is keeping your life and keeping you from becoming miserable. Someone may say, "Girl, how can you smile with all the problems you have?" If you know

Imam W. Deen Mohammed

scripture, you may quote some scripture to that person, for
this is life.

What is so special about a human being doing good, that they
can have that kind of protection from hell although they are
right in the midst of hell, but it is not touching them, thank
G-d. What is this all about? It is about the value of the human
being that G-d made. The human person was developing
upon the natural world; it was supporting human life.
The human being was developing materially, mentally and
everything was supporting that natural world that G-d, The
Creator, made before man came in with his influence and
changed it. He made it man's world and put man's creation all
around us.

We know the ground that we are looking at is just like G-d
made it; it hasn't changed. It's good to look at the ground. We
know the ground and the grass and the maintenance of those
things are the same as before man imposed himself upon G-
d's world. This doesn't mean that I'm against man's world. I
am in favor of it, but not of those things that hurt us.

None of us are completely pleased with man's world, but none of us want to do away completely with it, for man's world offers us a great abundance of good also. But at the same time, we have a thinking that will make us hurt ourselves and hurt society. We have to correct all of that. What I am talking about is going to help us to better situate ourselves inside of our own society. Even myself in putting this together strengthened me. Today, I am speaking on my favorite topic that shaped my life, the way I am today.

Those seers knew that there was going to come a time when every individual person would have much more responsibility than they had in the time of those seers. They believed that the city would not be able to guarantee you a good life, that it was going to become so burdened and so corrupt.

The cities that we built were formed so that we would have protection. That we would have support from our collective moneys and moral strength, etc. They supported cities, so that they would have a better life all together, with more streets, with more services and the store within a reasonable distance. They wanted a more comfortable and a safer, more secure life.

Finally, they had to get the police department and the fire department. But it was just to keep their life comfortable and secured with a sense of protection and a sense of being safe in the town. These cities have developed just as those seers of over 3,000 years ago were telling us. We see it now. The worst place to be is where people live. The safest place to be is where there are nothing but animals.

Originally, people wanted to be with other people and away from animals because then they were less protected. But now it is the other way around. today, we are much better off in the jungle with the animals and with a fire to keep them back.

The human being is not even tasty to animals. We have sweet meat, but it is not appealing to animals. Only the most vicious and the most hungry of animals will eat human meat.

The city is not supporting our life the way we wanted them to. We have the police and the fire department to come to our rescue, but they don't guarantee us security and protection. They can't do it anymore. The city is too burdened with too much corruption and insanity. The time is here that the seers saw.

The seers said that when this time comes, every person must accept more responsibility. We believe that day comes and night comes behind it, and behind night, day comes again. There is a returning of things.

The crescent moon comes and becomes a full moon and then there is no moon, and the new moon appears again. The sun comes and goes away. The storm may come, but the fair weather is coming behind it at some time. Everything is changing and repeating as in cycles.

So however we started, we are going to have to come back to that. This is what the great seers saw. We all started not depending upon city life, because there were no cities. We all started not depending upon the police department and fire department, because those things were not existing.

We were depending only upon our nature, our intelligence, our good hearts that G-d made us. We were made to make

selections. We don't just choose anything. We make
selections, and animals do too. But it is the free thought and
reason that we have and animals don't have, to think different
from the way we are created. We can come up with a new
idea of a way to live against the way we were created to live.
Animals can't do that. The animals can't think up another
lifestyle. The roach of today is the same as the roach during
the time of the Pharaohs of Egypt, who made them sacred
things. The dogs and birds and whatever it is living perform
the way G-d created them. It may have evolved slightly, but
it performs the same way. Its life is the same and its mold is
made, and it can't come out of that mold.

Only human beings were made to come out of their mold.
We should be thankful to What created us, that we were
created with more freedom than anything that exists.
We have more freedom than anything that exists, and look
what we have done with our freedom. We have made the city
a virtual hell in the life of most decent people. We have done
that with our freedom.

We couldn't have done that, if we were cockroaches and
bees. We would still be living in honey cones and life would

still be the same. This is prophesied that this would come. But I have said that things are returning, and we have to return to the way it was before.

We are not going to do away with these cities and the modern comforts we have; let's not be crazy people. We are going to keep all of these comforts, but in terms of how much of this responsibility I should accept in my own life for my own condition, we need a big change.

We cannot live in these cities anymore and say, "Well this is my house, my yard, and that is the extent of it for me. My job and this are the extent of my world." No, every step you take from your house, to your job is your world. Every step you go away from the job and the home, that is your world. Wherever you go on this planet, that is your world. This was true even way back when man had not created his world and there was nothing but the natural world that we say G-d made. G-d made all of this, and there is nothing except in man's history and in man's works that tell me this earth is not mine.

We paid for the ground we are standing on now, and we knew we had to pay for it. But this is what is on the minds of a lot of our youngsters right now. The world is pressuring our youngsters so much and making their lives so miserable, and they don't have the wherewithal and idea of how to cope with this thing. So then they depend on their own thinking. And what do they say: "Man says this is his, this town belongs to him. Man says I can't sleep on this ground, but this ground was made for all people and not just for The Man." So you have a movement against the System by these youngsters, who reject the whole System and condemn it. And they are not the first to do that, our African American young men and the Hispanics and others.

Back in the 1960s, it was the Ivy League high up White children who rebelled against the System. They were intelligent college students, who started living off the wild life and refusing to even go to stores and buy food. Their parents would have kept supporting them even in the way they were. But they were so much against the world as it was developing, that they decided they would reject the world and not accept anything from it.

Something causes you to go back. Enough pressure will cause you to go back. When we go back without guidance, we go back and down. But if we go back with guidance, we go back and up. I am speaking from Guidance; I am not speaking from Wallace.

We need to go back to the innocent human person. You want to know where that person is? It is in the arms of any new mother. The new baby that the mother gets into her arms, she gives to the father and they hold their future, the new human being. That new human being is ready to be guided aright. They use to have in the criminal laws that we had in the great United States of America, though it only stayed there temporarily -not for long, a law that allowed them to sterilize the really hardcore and bad criminals. They believed as scientists that criminology could be inherited. But science changed and brought back in the belief that "no, every child is born free of any criminal mind." They believed that no child was born with a criminal mind and had to stop that practice.

They would use the lie detector to sentence you or to let you go. It would deter-mine whether you go free or go to jail. It

would detect your own truthfulness. It was said you could lie with your tongue, with your mind, but your body, your flesh could not lie. They were putting things on to you that would reflect the life that G-d gave you and how it was affecting your thinking and your mind.

They would test you and find the lie detector going off, when they asked you certain things and could tell you when you were lying. What was it that was telling them that you were lying? It was the life that G-d gave you. You are in that life and you were lying in that body. Though as an adult you had become a criminal in your mind and a criminal in your behavior, that life had not changed.

Now, I think you can see what is the sacred human person in all the religions. For some, a person who is sacred like that and in agreement with their original innocence and purity, that person is also called "god." But for many religions, we say, "No, that person is not god. That is just a perfect person; not G-d."

We Paid For The Ground We Are Standing On Now

Every step you take from your house to your job is your world. Every step you go away from the job and the home, that is your world. Wherever you go on this planet, that is your world.

It is G-d Who looks for the perfect person who is like that, who still can appreciate and love and wants to obey his innocence that G-d created and wants to remain not guilty of any sins and any lies, G-d takes that person and makes him a messenger to direct others.

I heard a Christian Evangelist who I liked even before I met him, that is Dr. Robert H. Schuler with the TV Ministry from the Crystal Cathedral. I heard him teach once saying, "G-d believes in you." If He didn't believe in you, He wouldn't have trusted you to do the things that animals can't do. He must believe in you.

We have model human beings, not gods. No person is god, though G-d is present in all of us. Not only that, G-d is present everywhere. This is what our Scripture says and that of others. I know other Scriptures, too. But we don't like to think of G-d as being down, so when we think of G-d we look up. We like to think of Him being high up above all things imaginable. And I will do that myself. I will point one finger up, representing One G-d and to let someone know that that is where I am.

But for a scientist and astronomer, if you say straight up, he will tell you whatever it is won't be there for long. Because the earth is turning and even the sun will be in the shadow; the earth is blocking it. Then we see what is on the other side, the starry sky.

The poet says, "The night has a thousand eyes and the day one." With each quarter of the day passing, the sun is no longer straight up; it has moved down. If G-d is up there, then how long is He up there? So wherever we are and whatever situation we are in, we want to always respect G-d high above us in everything imaginable. He is not in any particular location.

I am trying to talk us into common sense, into the common intelligence that G-d created the baby with. Though we get away from that good common sense intelligence, when we get into this city life.

We need to get back to where we think with, good common sense. Think truthfully, think beauty and think love. The city is so much in our way, that we think ugly and think hate and sickness and violence. So let us come back to ourselves.

That is why the Honorable Elijah Muhammad called us the original man; he wanted us to think of our original selves and come back to that self.

Chapter 2

AL ISLAM WANTS EXCELLENCE FOR HUMAN BEINGS

Dallas, TX
April 27, 2004

With Allah's Name we begin, the praise and the thanks is for G-d. We thank Him for the gift and blessing of the model human person, Muhammed (pbuh), the honorable and noble servant and Messenger of G-d, and what follows of that salute or that traditional salutation to the last Prophet, the Seal of the Prophets mentioned in the Bible as it is given in the Qur'an.

We praise G-d, and we greet you with peace as Muslims say, As-Salaam Alaikum. It is really a pleasure and a great honor to address you here at this luncheon and to be invited by your Association of Professional Chaplains. And it is also a great plea-sure for me to see upon entering so many members of our association of Muslims you make me feel very happy and proud of you. Your presence here today is wonderful.

This is good experience for you and for us to sit at the table with these fine servants of G-d and mankind, to share food with them and to hear their voices and their minds. And I hope that you have done the same thing; I hope you have shared your voices and your minds at the tables with those who have invited and welcomed us here.

We begin with G-d's Name, the Merciful Benefactor, the Merciful Redeemer, or in the Name of G-d, the Beneficent, the Merciful, as it is translated in some translations of our Holy Book, the Qur'an.

I recall as a little boy younger than 11 years old, maybe 6 or 7 years old, my mother would dress me up real nice, and she would tell me, "I'm sending you to the Temple." I would go there, and I would hear the preacher preaching.

My father finally was able to come home from prison; I was about 14 years old. And he would open his lecture or his speech with, "Islam is Freedom, Justice and Equality." That was his habit over a period of 15 years or more, where he would open his speech like that - first with a prayer and then "Islam is Freedom, Justice and Equality."

That stuck with me and I think it helped form my sensitivities and also my interest. And today, I see the world of Islam and I think the whole world of Muslims need to understand Islam is Freedom, Justice and Equality.

Al Islam wants excellence for human beings, the same as Christianity, Judaism - all of our great religions want behavioral excellence for human beings, excellence of the human nature that we have, if there were conditions, circumstances to feed it and help us realize our excellence or experience growth of excellence for our human life, for our soul as human beings.

Al Islam Proclaims Man's Common Excellence

Proclaiming the excellence of man's common life, that is what Islam is, proclaiming the excellence of man's common life under G-d. That he should serve the community of mankind as a servant of G-d. What we perhaps need more than anything else in this world today is the innocence that G-d created us with and that all of us are born with.
Some of the organizations that I am a member of, when we meet the leaders often mention the need to achieve transparency.

We have in our Holy Book the saying, "Enter the door on hands and knees with the nose and forehead touching the floor." All of that is expressed in a little short phrase in Arabic "Enter the door or enter the gate in submission." But that is not enough, just to say in submission. I think when we describe it clearly and literally, it gives us the meaning as I have just given it to this honorable audience.

There is a growing awareness among these leaders, like the leaders of this organization that you mentioned me being a part of or a representative of The World Conference of Religions for Peace. And I have heard our leader, Dr. Bill Vinley, mention the need to achieve transparency.

There is hope for us and the world, as long as we have leaders in these organizations organized for peace, not only at home but peace everywhere on this planet earth and for justice everywhere on this planet earth.

We know we have many such servants serving mankind under G-d, as servants of G-d working alone or working with their friends in their neighborhoods or working with their associates, their colleagues. The world always has hope, as long as we have such persons who have achieved or are trying to achieve transparency.

The picture of world leaders today is shameful, and that is saying the least. Whether the picture we're looking at is the picture of the Asian world or European world or African world or the American people, we are looking at a very shameful picture.

I recall in my childhood, older women while they were observing the behavior of a child, they would say, "That boy is rotten to the core." Now we should never become rot-ten to the core.

We have in our Holy Book, the Qur'an, the saying, "Your death and your resurrection is liken to that of a single soul." The more our world works to mute human innocence, the more it gives itself to moral corruption of the human thought processes. Soon the loss of transparency brings on death of the whole society.

Business Life Will Be Void of Human Life

We know there are the living still walking the earth, but when we look at the general picture or the big picture, the picture of our publics and our leaders among them, it appears that we have allowed the whole society of man to lose human innocence, to lose transparency, openness, where you are not afraid to face your own secret thoughts and you are not ashamed if others see your own secret thoughts.

In time, if you lose this core that G-d created us with, business life will be void of human life. The approach to troubling issues won't have the support of this life that G-d gave us to save us in every area of life.

African American neighborhoods remain in their business life in infancy, because the leadership, I mean our leadership itself, is dead to man's original life that G-d gave us, when He put us in the Garden or put our Father in the Garden. I got this saying from Christianity, from the Bible. "Unless the children be reconciled...," now I understand it means the life. "Unless the children's life be reconciled with the life of the Father...." And I know Christianity perhaps and many Christians see this as reconciled with G-d. Yes, but it also is reconciled with Adam in his purity, before he lost it to the seducer.

Unless the children be reconciled in their life with the life of the father, the whole earth will be cursed. And when I look at our world today on television and what leaders are talking about, the violence and the trouble in our world, it seems as though the whole world is under a curse.

Selfish Promotion Invites Moral and Rational Death

Selfish promotion of one's own interest invites not only moral death but also the death of rational life as well. To work against moral life is stupid, not wisdom. Wisdom is not to see moral life separate from rational life.

We all know in these great heavenly religions, as we sometimes call them — Judaism, Christianity and Al Islam, we understand the fall of man, the fall of our Father Adam. It came only when he ate of a certain forbidden food and caused the generations to separate moral life from rational life or to see them separately.

Moral life will soon disappoint us, if it separates from rational life. And rational life will soon disappoint us, if it separates from moral thought or moral life. I believe that Al

Islam and Christianity are the same, in that we want to keep this life consistent, healthy and whole or complete.

In my conclusion, Muhammed the Prophet (pbuh) said, there will come a time when Jesus Christ and himself will be seen together. We believe in the birth of Jesus Christ without the help of man or without the involvement of a male. Maybe I cannot use the same language, the Immaculate Conception.

Al Islam and Christianity is separated not by knowledgeable people in these two religions, they are separated by people who have political interests. We have a scholar in Islam, Dr. Ibrahim Izzideen. He was giving an interview to the Focalore international movement of Catholics started by Chiara Lubich, who was experiencing as a child, as a young lady, a teenager about 17, the horrors of World War II, with bombs falling all around.

She decided to give her mind to Jesus Christ, peace be on him, as a servant, as a Catholic, as the person working hard to bring people to love one another, to call people back to Christ's Love. I became acquainted with her, meeting her through her book on her life, and I fell in love with her soul and her mind.

We formed a friendship, and that friendship now is a friendship for myself to those who are associated with me in the following and herself with those associated with her in her following.

The point I want to make here is that when we study these two religions with innocent hearts, as it says in our Book, "None can touch it." None can grasp the beauty and substance of the Qur'an, except the purified ones. When we are innocent in our hearts and minds and in our souls, we do not have any intentions that will shame us before G-d or the public, if we were to disclose those intentions. We have transparency, and G-d guides us to the substance and purity of our Scriptures.

I have read the Bible very carefully and very diligently. First I said to myself, "I want to be fair, I do not want to read the Bible and be picking it apart and questioning everything. I want to be able to go through the book like I want to. I vow that I will not stop to take anything apart or to question anything. I will read the Bible from cover to cover."

I did that, and G-d helped me do that. At the same time, when I was making the pledge to myself to do it that way, I also said, "And when I finish reading it that way, I'm going to pick it apart." And I did, but the first reading converted me to the purity of the Bible. I see a continuous line of purity from Genesis to Revelation.

So G-d put me in a situation where I could study it and look at it critically, and I did. So I have come to the conclusion that our religions want a world order that respects G-d and has man working in the service of mankind under G-d. G-d says He does not want anything from us; He needs nothing from us. He only wants from us our obedience.

Nations Allow Loss of Morals Will Hurt Masses and Leaders

In Al Islam, emphasis on behavior is very strong. Muslims are not to behave any kind of way. We can't follow the world of cultural trends that take us from life to death, back to life and then death. To me, nations that permit that kind of cultural life to control the lives of the masses of people and the leaders, also will fall victim to it. Because the common denominator for all of us is our moral life, our sensitive soul that G-d gave us, our emotions, etc. And no one is safe, no matter how educated we become, no matter how powerful we become. No one is safe from that danger of losing his soul, if we allow the influences that are against the health of the soul to take over the life of the public or the life of society.

In my opinion, we are no better than those ancient nations that regulated their societies by that kind of logic or that kind of insight into the nature of human behavior.
I believe that it is time for this great world that has advanced us in science and technology and also in human nature -we have become more socially mature because of the great advances we have made in the sciences and with our particular experience that we have with our democracy in the United States of America. So my prayer is that we study the society, study what governs our society and get the devil out of our society.

Peace to you, As Salaam Alaikum.

Imam W. Deen Mohammed

Chapter 3

ISLAM COMES TO AWAKEN US FOR COMMUNITY LIFE

Brooklyn, NY
May 17, 2002

We begin with G-d's Name, Who is merciful to us, The Merciful Benefactor and Merciful Redeemer. That is, He is merciful to us twice for our life here and hereafter. Firstly, He is merciful to us by creating us in such a wonderful human form and creating us with a mind and intellect to enjoy the material world, both with our bodies and with our minds or with our material life and our spiritual life.

Then He is merciful to us again, when we lose the way and can't see any further how to carry our life where we want it to go, He gives us revelation or guidance through one who deserves that special help from G-d, our Creator. And we are put into a good position again to start afresh with our life and to carry it where our souls want it to go, where G-d wants it to go.

G-d has put it in the soul that He created to know where to go. That is, if we clean our minds and hearts and have nothing deceitful in us and be not all for ourselves but for our community, G-d will let us know through our souls where we should take our lives.

We witness that G-d is One Alone. It means that He does not need anyone or anything to help Him manage His creation, all of it, the skies and earth and everything therein. He has no partner or god with Him; He is G-d Alone. If anyone comes to Him, according to His Words in Qur'an, he comes as a servant.

We know all of the Prophets in Bible and Qur'an are written as servants of G-d, including Jesus Christ, peace be upon him, and all the Prophets and Messengers of G-d. Jesus introduced himself as a servant to G-d, in the Bible. And G-d says to Muhammad (pbuh), revealing the Qur'an for the world, no one comes to Him except as a servant, not as a god or equal with Him.

G-d says in Qur'an, "I need not for you to feed Me (G-d)." He slumbers not and takes no sleep; He feeds but is not fed. That is G-d, the Creator. And we witness that Muhammad (pbuh), to whom the Qur'an was revealed over 1,400 years ago, is His Servant and His Messenger. That is our creed, our declaration of faith.

Our faith is firstly in G-d, Who created everything and made possible all goodness and all good things. Secondly, our faith is in man. When we say that we witness that Muhammad (pbuh) is the Messenger of G-d and the Last Prophet, we are saying that we have faith in G-d and in man. G-d requires that we not only have faith in G-d, but that we have faith also in man.

So it is not good just to believe. We are to look at Muhammad the Prophet (pbuh) and see him in his personal life as a human being and in his life as a prophet, for he is also for us a sign, as Jesus was a sign, peace be upon them. He is a sign that G-d does not need man to get man where He wants man to go.

The whole world can fail the human being. The whole world can fail the human soul. But that does not mean that G-d is helpless and depending on man to carry the human soul to where He wants it to go. When all of their knowledge runs out and can't help us, when all of their creations can't help us, when all of their teaching and preaching can't help us, G-d can revive the intellect of the human being and lift that intellect up to higher planes, where that intellect will experience revelation on the highest level and come into a much bigger focus and dimension of his reality.

Then G-d will cause him to come back down off the high plane or level that He lifted him up to back with his people on the ground and revive them and guide them, so they will have what their souls call for. G-d never did anything stupid! G-d never did anything that was senseless! Whatever G-d did, it is intelligent. Whatever G-d did makes sense. Understand that, firstly.

We must respect G-d. G-d doesn't play. G-d doesn't stroke Himself. He doesn't need that; we need that. We don't have to believe in a G-d that needs us to worship Him; He doesn't need us to worship Him. He is not a G-d that needs us to thank Him; He doesn't need us to thank Him. A G-d that needs us to pray to Him and bow down to Him or glorify Him, G-d doesn't need that at all.

But G-d created us and we are His creation and His creation needs to obey the Creator. And the creation needs to acknowledge the Creator The creation needs to appreciate the

Creator. The more the creation does that, the better the creation is; it becomes better and better.

It is for us that we have revelation. It is for us that we have prayers. G-d does not need our prayers; we give G-d nothing when we pray to Him. Muhammed the Prophet (pbuh) said: "You cannot increase G-d by any little small bit by whatever you want to do for Him. This is what the Prophet (pbuh) taught to us. He is already perfect. And when He created the world, He didn't create it for Him to feed on it. He didn't create the world for the world to give Him strength. He created the world for man - the whole world, everything.

The sky and everything up there and the earth and everything down here, the insects and smallest things in creation, G-d did not create that for G-d. G-d created that for us, man. And man is the only creature that we see finding joy, pleasure, usefulness in everything that G-d created. Nothing that G-d created is without use to human beings and community life.

We have the Museum of Science and Industry in Chicago. There we have all kinds of insects and things on display, as well as technology. We see all the animals. We have courses

taught now in our schools. No matter how small life is, plant or animal, it is of interest to us. But isn't it true that G-d created all of this for man?

Nothing else wants to know about all these things. It is only man who wants to know all these things and seems to bring all of these things into his environment to study them, to ponder over them, to find enjoyment in them. So the world and all things, as the Prophet (pbuh) has taught us and the Prophets before taught us, all things that you see or know of in this world are created for man.

G-d needed nothing. We should first know G-d as The Real G-d, then we will have real faith, strong faith, undying faith. Then we will have strong interest, undying interest in the mission. Without these things brought to your mind and conscience, religion for you is like passing through a flower garden.

As long as the wind is blowing the beautiful smell in your nose, there is pleasure in passing through the flower garden. But there is a stockyard close by and if the wind changes, you will be passing through the flower garden, but you are smelling the stockyard.

That is how religion is in this world. As soon as something bad comes into their nose or senses, they lose the good relationship or good experience in religion. It should not be that way. Your mind should be converted to G-d. Islam is the only religion that I know of that insists upon your mind being converted to G-d.

We say, "I witness." 'I witness" is given also in the Bible. But it was not established by the followers of the Bible, except for a few. Muhammed the Prophet (pbuh) came to say it is important, that your mind and your intelligence convert to G-d not just your spirit and your soul. Your mind and your intelligence should witness this Truth, that G-d is Creator of everything. G-d is G-d, and G-d has lifted up man; not only created him, but lifted him up in his intellect so that he will be a guide for the whole world of mankind.

The place for us to start is in the heart, but we are not just creatures of the heart. The animals have hearts and sometimes they display sentiments of the heart that attract our attention. We will be amazed and it touches our heart from their hearts. But I don't think any of them can touch us with their intellects, with their minds like we can touch each other with our minds. We are superior to all created things, in our minds and in our intelligence.

G-d created a human being and gave that human being a superiority over other creatures and life He made, and that superiority is not in his feelings, not in his heart but in his intellect, in his mind.

So would He be a G-d making sense, if He didn't establish that human being in his intelligence and if He didn't tell them to develop their minds and cultivate their minds and respect their human intelligence and to use the tools of intelligence for their future good and benefit and conscience.

If He didn't do that, He would not even make sense after making the human being like that and then ignore the great wealth and value that He gave that creature when He gave him reasoning, intelligence and intellect.

So when you say, "I witness that there is but One G-d," you are supposed to say that with rational sense. And there is plenty rational guidance in the Qur'an that forces us to the conclusion that there is a G-d over all this creation. And that, that G-d is not two or three or four or many, that that G-d is One. The creation itself points to One G-d, not to more than one.

That is the rational conclusion you should make. And if you don't have that when you come to Islam, when you hear the teachings of Islam, when you read the Qur'an, you should be guided to that kind of conclusion. And when you take your Shahadah or Declaration of Faith, it should be from the intellect, not from the heart and spirit.

This religion prepares us to accept responsibility for the community life of man on this planet earth.

This religion prepares us to accept responsibility for the community life of man on this planet earth. The great messengers and teachers of G-d come from mankind and they put mankind in the right position and on the right road. But in time, because man is encouraged by religion to engage

the world so that it becomes a better world as a home for the human soul, or in trying to protect the human soul, man gets too involved in material things and things of the flesh and forgets what he was given from the messenger or the prophet that started him on the road.

Pretty soon, he is so far lost that he has to have another messenger or revivalist or someone to bring him back to where he is supposed to be. This happens, it has happened and will continue to happen. Muhammed the Prophet (pbuh) prophesied that his community would go down and fall under darkness, but it would be revived.

He promised his community, and that is us we are his community and all of the people who follow the Qur'an and Islam knowing that it was revealed to Muhammed the Prophet (pbuh); there are over 1 billion of us now on this earth in most of the countries of the world.

Muhammed the Prophet (pbuh) told us that at the head of every 100 years, there would be someone to revive the religion. Now if he said these things, should we be thinking that the Islamic world is all right all the time? How can it be all right all the time, if the Prophet (pbuh) said it was going to go into darkness, even after he had guided it right; he had set it up correctly?

He himself said it was going to go down. He himself said that at the head of every 100 years, there would be someone to revive it, a mujeddid, to bring back the newness or freshness, as it was before.

So we shouldn't then think that the Islamic world is in good shape all of the time, if what he said is correct. There are going to be times when the whole Islamic world is under darkness and not finding its way. But we shouldn't give up hope, because he said that there would come at the head of every 100 years a revivalist. What is he saying?

Do you think you can watch your calendar and say, "It's a hundred years at this moment, brother. The revivalist is here." No, that is not how it works. In the Arabic language, Islam is science, Islam is revelation, Islam is language that is on the level of the common man and at the same time is much higher than the grasp of the common man.

You need a special man inspired by G-d at times, or sometimes it is a woman, who will get us back to where we are supposed to be in our thinking. When the thinking is corrected, the thinking then can correct the heart. But when the thinking is in the dark, all we can depend on is the heart, and at first the heart is innocent and good.

When Muhammad (pbuh) said "every 100 years," it has to be translated or interpreted. The word in Arabic for 100 is "niat" and a death is "miat." These two words have the same essential constitution, when it comes to lettering. So when the Prophet (pbuh) said a hundred years, it was a play on "death."
Whenever his community dies, there is going to be one to resurrect it. Whenever this community dies to the right perception and way to live and practice Islam, there will be one to revive that understanding, to give it life again.

And the call to prayer begins with the word "life." First, we acknowledge G-d, that He is more important than anything else. Then you say, "Come to Prayer." That is the first pronouncement of the Call. The word is "Hayya," which is used to call someone and it means living.

The Arabs did not just hear that word for the first time from Muhammad's (pbuh) mouth. There is an Arab proverb in the Bible that says: "A living dog is better than a dead lion." In this proverb is the word "hayya," the living. In the Call to Prayer, "hayya" is given as an imperative or as an order. It is a noun and a verb, for example the word "stop" is a noun and a verb.

"Hayya" in Arabic is living as in a noun. If you say, "Hayya alas salat," the same word that meant living now means "come." To the enlightened student who is searching language for more knowledge and understanding, this is saying to that student that this word does not merely mean "come," it means "come with enthusiasm, come living - not dead or sleepy or slumbering or absentminded." It means come with enthusiasm, come lively to prayer.

What is prayer now? To know this makes the difference between a live Muslim and a dead Muslim. When you see Christians with their hands up, they are praying. That is not the way we pray. When you see Muslims have their hands up, that is the way we beg not the way we pray. This is saying that we are begging our G-d; we are not supposed to beg man.

The Prophet said the one who holds his hand out begging is inferior to the one who gives to the hand. To hold the hands out in prayer for the Muslim is not salat; this is du'a. And du'a means to call for help. To understand prayer in Islam, we must get the understanding from revelation, from the Qur'an and Muhammad (pbuh). But the first source is revelation.

In the Qur'an, Allah (swt) says every creature knows its mode of prayer. The lion, the eagle, the snake, the mosquito, the fly - it didn't leave out any. It says that every creature knows its mode of prayer.

So what then is prayer? Prayer is your natural life's discipline given to you by Creator. All the animals that G-d didn't give free will and free intellect or mind, they stay in the same mold created for them by their Creator; they don't come out of that mold.

They wake up like they are supposed to wake up. They go to sleep like they are supposed to sleep. They move and transport themselves like they are supposed to - as they were created to. They form their families and their societies as they were created to. They conduct their daily life to survive as they were created to do it.

Man is above them in creation. Man is created also to think and plan his future. But the same G-d that gave that mold for them, gave us also our thinking mold and He has planned thought in human life to take us from animal existence to inspired man's existence and to serve community in a way to make it the most excellent and the most trouble free and intelligent community, the most obedient community to G-d, to Creator.

It is to be the strongest sign that this community recognizes its Creator and gives credit to its Creator above all things. This G-d has created our intellect to acknowledge Him and to take our life to the best possible condition. This G-d has given this to us in our nature, in our souls and in our minds. This will happen in a natural way. That is what Allah (swt) says to us through Muhammad (pbuh) and revelation, "it is the religion of origin" our human origin, that He has pattern the human civilized society of man upon. So we think of revelation and yes, we need revelation just to assist evolution when man runs out.

G-d says, "My man is ready for Me now. He has run out. He knows not where to take his life. He has learned that he will fail himself. Now I will come and help you. So he will know Me." G-d wants to be known by human beings, so that human beings can do more with His creation than animals can do.

G-d wants this creation to be better, and He created one of the animals to do that with the capacity and potential to go higher and reach further with his mind and to take His creation further than animals can take it. He wants it taken to community life. This is where you should be in your thinking.

We, the world of religious teachers, are so far behind. We are talking to man's soul, we are talking to his spirit but are doing little teaching to his rational mind. And that is a big mistake.

In Islam, the focus is the rational mind and Muhammed the Prophet, peace be upon him, said "G-d did not create anything better than the human brain." This is the saying of our Prophet (pbuh) recorded in Bukhari and Muslim in hadith, the great volumes of information.

Now if G-d wants me to glorify Him, should I just glorify Him with my hands in clapping or just by shouting with noise and movement. A king may invite me to perform for him and I know how to crack jokes and dance and sing, but I also have mental skills and can do calculus and the kingdom doesn't have calculus. If he invites me, should I offer him what is superior or what I have that is inferior? Should I buck dance when the king needs calculus and I know calculus?

Should I go and give G-d the spirit of my soul and the sentiments of my heart, when G-d has created my brain above my soul and above my heart. Although the soul is so mysterious, it may extend above my brain, but I do know it waits on my brain to do something. So should I perform with my spirit and not perform with my mind for G-d? Should I glorify Him with my spirit and not with my intelligence?

When you see what has happened in this world to bring communities from existing just like animals, eating, sleeping, having sex, playing and dying, to engage in the material world and to give human beings science and technology and many comforts with the intellect working with matter....

When you see that, know that G-d created human beings to glorify Him

When you see how Islam came in the time of Muhammad (pbuh), when the world had left off intellectual interest and scientific inquiries, when Muhammad (pbuh) received Qur'an, it was inspired again in the minds of studious men and women. Then the great sciences and technology came back -medicine, astronomy with instruments to study the stars, with instruments to make glass; all of this came back. Then came universities and colleges.

When you see that, know that G-d created human beings to glorify Him, not just with the instruments of their feelings but with the instrument of their brain and their rational faculties, etc. This is a great glorification.

"G-d, return me to the womb of science and knowledge and direction from You, so I can stand up as a living man on my feet again." So we glorify G-d and say, "G-d, I lost it, but I'm giving it back to You. I think I have found myself, and I am going to put my head on the ground that You took me out of, in hope that I will be born again and live again and glorify You with my whole life and with my mind."

Then educate your brothers. Educate your sisters. Educate your public for a better world. This is prayer. That is why on the Jumuah Day we don't have to say four rakat of Thuhr, the mid-day prayer. We cut it in half, because what I am doing with my khutbah (speech) is prayer.

The Bible has Jesus saying, "Give us this day our daily bread." He wasn't talking about Wonder Bread from the store. He was talking about the <u>b-read</u> - to be read and read correctly. And I need it daily." Is there proof of this in the Bible? Yes. The Bible said of Jesus, "Take this in the communion [wine] in the remembrance of Me."

The Bible says that the wine represents spirit and that it is the spirit of the New Testament. "Take this bread in

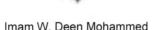

remembrance of me, my body." And the Bible tells us that this bread is the doctrine of the New Testament. Doctrine means teachings.

The wine represents spirit, and the bread represents teachings. So I say to you to take the "b" off of bread and just read it as "read." This is in agreement with the New Testament. This is a wonderful loaf of bread. In fact, it is five-in-one. Here is what we should be looking at. Islam comes to awaken us for community life. Muslims can't be Muslims on an island somewhere off to ourselves, away from our society and away from our people.

Muslims are obligated by the teachings of Islam to establish the individual in community; not outside of community. All of our aspirations, all of our hopes -you are to first look at your community and then pick a place in your community for you to establish yourself upon or in. This is Islam. Islam requires that of us.

We are not to go out on our own individually and try to make a life for ourselves. We have to look at our community first and plan our life with respect to what our community gave us, with respect for what our community needs and with respect for where our community has to go in order to meet what G-d asks of community in Qur'an and in those teachings on the life of Muhammed the Prophet (pbuh).

G-d Also Says That We Are Created Like A Plant

Islam is community life, not just living our own life privately or selfishly. Islam comes to do what civilization does. When we are told by G-d that this is a community of "fitrah," a community of origin, archeologists and the sciences that study the past life of man on this earth find evidence that human life is an evolving life.

G-d also says that we are created like a plant. And just like a plant starts with a seed and develops itself upon a stem and later produces a beautiful design or symmetry or production and oftentimes produces something useful to other life -seeds or fruits that other life feeds upon, including human beings or beauty that the human soul feeds on, it is giving something.

When the plant establishes itself, it is giving to something other than itself. The simplest of plants that has no seed, no fruit, no nuts, no beauty, it will die and its dead body enriches the soil that it came up out of or was taken from. It makes the soil richer for itself and for other things to grow in. **G-d has created life not to live selfishly but to give unselfishly, charity.**

Some of the greatest advancements we have made for human society have been made possible because of people not being selfish. Because if we were selfish, we would not even give the knowledge freely; not to mention the material benefits that some of us are fortunate to have and share with others so they would have a better life.

We wouldn't have the knowledge and the sciences in the world making it so beautiful, if it weren't for the charity that is in the heart of every human being. This is the beauty of religion; this is the substance of religion. The substance of religion is not in show, not in rituals, not in dressing up in your ihram, the two pieces of cloth, and bringing your picture back from Hajj to show people.

The substance of this religion is not "Allahu Akbar," and nobody heard it. These people are dead; you have to teach them for them to hear that. Just like it is for the evolution of man, social science believes that man has a natural desire and urge in him to evolve. To get better and better, more developed and more developed, become more resourceful and more resourceful, to become more qualified to do greater and better things. Science says that man is created with this spirit and desire in him to evolve socially.

Science says that civilization does not really present itself, until man perceives his social aim of where he should take his life in community with other men and people and families; not just his private life. He has to be turned on to where he is to take his community life, his people, his tribe that he lives with on this earth or continent or peninsula. When he gets in that mind, that is when he starts to evolve socially.

This takes him to his social aim. That is to have comfort not just for himself but for the people he belongs to. If your Imam W. Deen Mohammed were not turned on to this when he was a teenager, you would not have W. Deen Mohammed. It is not the Qur'an and the Sunnah that made this Imam. It is my desire to live the best of my social nature and to follow the best aim in this social nature, so that our people and I will be helped by my existence. Elijah Muhammad, my father, turned that on in me.

It was because of that nature, my "fitrah" that I was given that, and I was able to guide you to the Qur'an and the Sunnah. I know where my salvation is. I know where my savior was, in my "fitrah."

To succeed in this world where all human beings have the same nature; G-d gave every human being a "fitrah." To compete in this world and to succeed, we need a strategy and a superior strategy, because other people have strategies too. We need the best strategy that can compete with all other strategies and not be defeated. That is the strategy of Islam. That is the strategy Muhammad (pbuh) had, prayers and peace be upon him.

The best strategy is the one of openness, not secrecy. G-d loves Truth. G-d loves courage in a righteous man, a righteous man who is brave enough to trust Truth, even when falsehood tells him he can live longer. But don't think this is a silly, foolish openness. This is a wise openness. It reveals itself to those on top first, before the middleman hears it. It is put in a language that escapes the man on the ground but reaches the man in the high tower.

They now say: "Uh oh, we have company and we didn't create him. He is telling everything and telling what we are doing up here. We have to review our work and see where we are right now and see if we have done anything wrong. We have to make sure we are on solid ground. See if there is a prediction we can work out to explain this guy's creation." So they go back and study.

Then they come up with the conclusion: "He has seen in the sanctuary and into the sacred quarters, but he is not guided by G-d. He lacks the wisdom that G-d gives. So let's ignore him. Let's embarrass him. Let's bring out his weak side. Let's destroy him." But if they say, "he is genuine, he is wise, he is protected by G-d," they are quiet as they can possibly be. Because everything they say, they know he is going to hear it.

Chapter 4

WAKE UP TO HUMAN LIFE

Homewood, IL
January 2, 2005

We say Allahu Akbar meaning G-d is greater than anything imaginable. We greet you on this second day of the New Year and by the way we wish you all blessed New Year. We praise G-d the Lord and Cherisher of all the worlds. All that is in the sky and all that is down here. We witness that He is One and He cares about all of His creation and His special creation of human beings. We witness that Muhammad (pbuh) is the Seal of the Prophets, the last Prophet.

We are grateful Allah (swt) for our health and our presence here to address the radio listening audience and we appreciate you tuning into this occasion.

We praise G-d the Lord, Sustainer of the worlds. He is Most Merciful. The Merciful Benefactor, the Merciful Redeemer or as it is translated the Beneficent, the Merciful and the Compassionate, the Merciful. He is Ar Rahmaan Ar Raheem. Those are the two names that we translate and both meaning the G-d of Mercy. Mercy firstly in that He gave us the life we have, He made us human and He made the world to support our life. And He says that He has made the earth to give us everything that we need for our life. All of our aspirations can be fulfilled on this earth, praise be to Allah (swt).

We are addressing life in community, how we are to build up our communities so that our souls will be pleased. The human souls cannot be pleased unless you do what you're created to do, then your soul will be pleased. But as long as you have not fulfilled to do what you were created to do or created for, then your soul will not be happy and you can't be happy if your soul is empty, sad, in pain or hurting.   G-d wants us to care about ourselves, to value ourselves. Nothing communicated to man or brought to us as education or news, has respected our value as G-d has respected our value.

In the world today there are publics, populations. Their way of thinking is influenced by Judaism, Christianity and Al Islam. There are other publics influenced by Buddhism, Hinduism and many other religions, the great majority of people on this planet are influenced by those major religions. And all of these religions place great value on the human person and they invite the human person to wake up to the human value that they have by virtue of their creation, that they were created human. If you were created human, you have special possibilities for your life that are not open to any other life except human life.

And all of these religions place great value on the human person and they invite the human person to wake up to the human value that they have by virtue of their creation, that they were created human. If you were created human, you have special possibilities for your life that are not open to any other life except human life.   Not even the angels according to revelations have the freedom that human beings have. The angels do not have the freedom to alter creation and re-create and get the great satisfaction in their souls, spirit and minds of doing things worthwhile, beautiful and helpful to society, not only of the community of the family of man, but to the community of animals as well.

Man has made history and if you study history you will see that man has made progress. If you go get a book that is a thousand years old and look at the human environment, its miseries, diseases, etc., and look at it now, you will see that man has made progress. If you get a history book and read of what was existing for us just two or three hundred years ago, you'll see we have made progress. I have been living as a

Chicagoan for most of my life and I know Chicago seventy years ago. When I was a baby in Chicago that is not the Chicago that I look at now, it was a backwards city, when I look at the city of Chicago now. Traveling around in the city was not as convenient as it is now, the smell of the air was not as nice as it is now because horse drawn vehicles were going down the street and horses were dropping their waste on the street and you could smell that sometimes if you walked or drove down the streets.

So man is making progress. How are we making progress? We're making progress by building upon that work that others did before us. Building upon that which was good for human life that others left with us. Building upon the progress in the material environment that others left with us. Fathers and mothers passing on their life story of their mothers and fathers. Passing it on to their children, passing on the wisdom and the good advice, passing on the good nature to their children, this is how we have made progress. If we stop doing that then we will not have progress. We start to go backwards instead of forward, we start to go down instead of up, this is life and this is history. So let us all recognize this. Become aware of these things and think seriously about life. Don't make a joke of life, don't take life for a joke. Don't make your life a life of play. You're not babies anymore I'm looking at an audience here of mostly grownups, very few children are in here.

Very few babies are in here that I am looking, so don't make your life a life of play. G-d gave us play to train us for an adult life and adult responsibilities. When you play you use your muscles, reflexes, your endurance and that is building you up to be able to have a good job and manage it and not get tired so fast. It is building you up to have muscles for a life of adult responsibility. So don't take play in children for fun, no. It is fun alright but G-d gave that fun to teach the children skills that they will need for an adult life of adult responsibility, we should understand these things and wake up. We should prepare ourselves to live in a world that offers a human being much more, than the world of the past offered human beings.

We should be thankful to G-d for that, if we don't believe in G-d we should thank whatever we imagine is responsible for that. The point is to be thankful, be grateful, be appreciative and when you do that, your soul will like you more, but when you don't do that, your soul won't even like you and it will make you destroy yourself because your soul wants to see you punished. Your own soul hates that you disrespect the wonderful creation that G-d has made you. No other creature has been made free to manage its own life and manage his or her own nature, no other creature has been made free to do that. The animals can't manage their own nature, they can only live within and under their own nature, but a human being can manage his own nature. You can take your nature into your own hands as your responsibility and you can improve upon your own nature. Every child that is born eventually crawls around on all fours like animals, no matter how beautiful the baby, no matter how high the parents were in cultural development or whatever. The baby comes here lying and crawling around like an animal not able to speak the language, it learns the language from us.

According to those who study the development of society, scientists, they say if you leave the child alone and not have it supported by intelligent human beings, if it is found by animals and lives with animals, it will think itself an animal and it will try to behave and speak, make sounds like the animal that it survives among.

This is history, it has shown us that. So don't think that G-d wants you to stay on all fours. He created you to stand up on your two feet. There are monkeys, apes and other primates that stand up on two feet. And there are some birds that stand up on two feet. I like to watch the penguins do their little shuffle, they walk on two feet. To stand on two feet is not enough, but that is a start, you have to elevate yourself. We learn from the wisdom of the ancient, by way of revelation that if you care about yourself and you invest in yourself, you spend time on making your nature better, making your intelligence better, you spend time on making your morals better, if you spend on your own self to increase your own value you can become the person who can bring relief and happiness, cleanliness, civilization, education. You can bring the beautiful life that we imagine now in this time.

We're Very Special People

Don't you know it was just a few thousand years ago human beings couldn't even imagine living like we live now? They had no education, no science, no evidence that would give them that kind of mind and thinking, that they would think like we think with the opportunities that we're looking at and be able to proceed, go forward with our life like we can go forward with our lives. So we're very special people in spite of all of the trouble you're facing and all of the bad news you're getting by way of television and whatever, we are blessed to be on this earth at this particular time and sometimes it takes natural disasters to wake some of us up.

Look how the people who suffered that quake in the ocean, the tsunami, seeing a wave thirty feet high coming at them, that is frightening, that is enough to wake up the real person in that body and maybe that is what we need to happen to us sometimes.

A great tragedy, to wake up the human person in our body, because most of us are not respecting the human person in our own body and we wonder how come we have so much trouble, we're suffering so much, how come drugs are being taken by everybody, because those bodies are only flesh, the human being is gone. Bring the human being back into those bodies and you will see a difference in the way they behave before the temptations of drugs, of violence.

When the human is in the body the way he or she is supposed to be in the human body, we can handle the temptation of drugs, to become violent, the temptation to put our burden on everybody else, to go out and pour our misery on the public traffic. We drive so you get somebody killed, deny them the opportunity to make a left turn at the corner, this is what is going on, rudeness and cruelty on the streets. Motorists out to make another motorist miserable, this is a sad time for the state of human life, in the human body.

So come back home, have the human mind. Come back into those human bodies you have and appreciate that G-d has made you more valuable than any other living thing. We degrade ourselves, we put ourselves down when we mistreat human life especially our own.

We never should take our own life, only G-d should say when we die not us. We don't say when we die. We didn't say when we should be born and we shouldn't say when we die, that is G-d's right and we take a right from G-d and we have to be punished for that if we do that. We know that is terrible. But what is worse than that, are those committing suicide taking drugs, beating up on people, killing people.

They are committing suicide because eventually somebody is going to beat up on them and kill them and they are dying fast. Millions are dying all over the planet earth because of insane behavior, so this is a suicide that is ugly. Let us wake up! It is wake up time.

We should want to know something about this fine life that G-d has given to only humans, every religion that I know of that is practiced or lived by, great numbers of persons on this earth they attend that need to bring to the consciousness of their following human values so that they will respect human life and the society can make progress. We cannot make progress if you don't respect human life. If we respect human life we can make progress. If you don't respect human life in your home, you may be in your apartment or you may be in your own house but if you have members there sharing that environment, sharing that space, if they don't respect human life, that space will be made a hell for all the members occupying that space. It is no different for the town or the city. If the people are not respecting human life, then their behavior is going to make a hell for the rest of us, a hell for everybody.

Really, that is what life is in most of the quarters of these big cities, it is a virtual hell. The suffering that goes on this earth today it doesn't look any less frightening to me than what I learned that hell has for those who are going to hell. Hell is a place where you are burned and will not be burned up.

I see families miserable, mothers miserable, grandparents miserable seeing their sons and daughters on drugs going to the graveyard. Violent prone, sick with immorality, sick with moral corruption, they're looking at that and can't do anything about it. That is hell fire, that is a fire that burns all the time. It burns and won't stop burning and we're living in it and we're not burned up. We just burn, burn, burn with no end coming in sight we think.

We can turn that thing around, bring the human being back in the body and we will see a great difference, that is what religion is all about. Religion is not about you shouting and pretending holiness, fainting and carrying on, then go out leaving the church, the temple or the mosque and go right back to the same life of self destruction making others and yourself miserable, that is not religion. Religion is beautiful, it is intelligent, it respects human life so much that it wants

us to have the intelligence to manage human life for
ourselves.

This is Al Islam, this is Christianity, this is Judaism, this is
Buddhism, this is Hinduism. Every religion wants you to
have the intelligence to manage your own life, to manage
your own self and to get the satisfaction of seeing your life
progress knowing that your actions, your behavior is what
made that happen.

I came up in bad neighborhood circumstances and I'm not
the only leader who is doing well who came up in bad
circumstances. I was a child and could walk two blocks and
run into a prostitute or a wine head. Sometimes I didn't have
to walk anywhere, as soon as I stepped outside there was a
prostitute or a wine head or sometimes the drug addict or
people who didn't care about themselves. They were victims
of the instruments of the devil like drugs, whiskey etc., now
we're victims of the instruments of our own selves.

We're not hooked on drugs, we're not so poor that we have
to drown our misery with alcohol, we live in nice apartments,
we have color televisions, we're doing very well, but still the

human life is not respected. We are mistreating our own human life, mistreating the lives of other human beings near us, our loved ones, our friends, our relatives. Parents abandoning their responsibility to their children and I'm not talking about responsibility to see that they have food on the table or to see that they have clothes to wear, the greater responsibility is to see that they have good sense, to see they have intelligent human behavior.

Parents are abandoning that responsibility and letting the children do their own thing and saying, "What can you do, everybody is doing it?" I'm telling you, those who think they don't go to hell by themselves or with a whole lot of company you're wrong, you don't have company when you go to hell, you go to hell alone. And if you have company it increases the hell so you're still alone. Hell will surprise you, in fact I think it surprised most of you already because you don't even know you're in hell, it slipped up on you.

There are some religions that believe hell and heaven start in this life while we're physically living on this earth, my religion is one of those religions that believes that hell starts in this life and heaven starts also in this life, but you don't get the fullness of either until this life goes away. Then you will wake up in another reality and then you will get the fullness of your good life or the fullness of your bad life, it will be completed for you.

This is a belief that is in at least two of the major religions that I'm aware of and maybe more than that. There are not many religions that are leading the public's of the world today. The religions that you do not know of and there are many, thousands of them, they have very few followers. They don't have big followings, the big followings belong to the major religions, Judaism, Christianity, Al Islam, Buddhism, Hinduism. These major religions, they have the majority of the people in the publics of the world.

Can we say the state of the world is to be blamed on these religions? I know these religions and I can read the beauty of the various religions, I can read any of those book and I am put in a mind to respect what I'm reading, appreciate what I'm reading and put great value on what I'm reading. So if I can go to these religions, go to their Holy Books and read and get this kind of feeling, and lift in spirit, it lifts my spirit.

When I see their beauty and their wisdom, their good, pure purpose, when I see it makes me feel good, it makes me happy and I am soothed by what I read. So it is not the fault of these religions, it is the fault of their public's, the public goes astray from the religions and we as individuals get weak for the public life and we leave the good teaching, the good family or good parents and we join the public life and go to hell.

The public life, especially in the modern world or industrial world, is a life that lets you know right away it is all about money. You step out in the public, you see people trying to get your money. As soon as you step out there and you see some activity in the public, most likely it is somebody trying to get your money. In our neighborhood, in certain quarters we live in, as poor folks, people who have lost the respect for human life. We come out in our neighborhood and we can't hardly find a dog, they are disappearing. I used to see a lot of dogs when I was a boy.

In order for us to appreciate human life we have to appreciate community life. There is no way to appreciate your human, individual life without you and us appreciating community life. G-d didn't make us to live outside of community, He made us to live in community. He didn't make us to go with the mind that "Life is all about me." G-d made us to go with the mind that life is indebted to my family, life is indebted to my community, life is indebted to my city, my state my nation, that is how G-d makes us.

He makes us with intelligence to appreciate life in community and to understand that is the only way you can have life. Somebody might say, "I don't want nothing. I'd rather be by myself." What about the electricity, what about the water, heat for the house and telephone are you going to do all of that by yourself? Can you bring all that into your house and to yourself and by yourself? No. the reality is that you do not ever live alone, you always live the life of community and if you didn't have community life you wouldn't be able to survive alone you would have nothing but bare earth. And I don't think this pampered generation that we have today can survive on the bare earth, you would go out there and cut your throat quick or look for something to kill yourself with quick saying, "I can't make it, where am I going to stay tonight? Under a tree, up on a branch?" If you are afraid some dogs are going to get you, climb up a tree up high on a branch, hug the branch and go to sleep. You won't be able to sleep too long you will sleep a minute or so and then wake up.

Some of us are against government and everything, it is all corrupt and when we look at you we see corruption. You reject the world and everything. Well try living without anything but yourself.

The big world is out there if you think you can find some seeds from an apple or something or seeds from corn and plant it and have the patience to wait for it to grow and then get out there and gather it. Go out there, work and bring it in, take it into your yard where there is no house, no grass and get some dry wood. Build yourself a fire, do you think you can cook it and survive like that? No. You don't have the spirit and endurance to meet the challenge of a natural environment without man's work in it. Wake up and let us appreciate life more, living in community more. Let us realize we owe community life for the things that we enjoy on this planet earth. Whoever is responsible for the community, the neighborhood, we owe them.

The government that protects the order of the neighborhood and city. We owe that order. We pay taxes, we pay for that, you are supposed to. That is a service to all of us. Don't be angry because you have to pay taxes, be angry because your taxes are not directed properly or used in the best manner or the best way. Don't tear down the system, correct the things that are wrong for the system and help the things that are right for the system. The system managed to give us an environment wherein we can live as human beings and feel comfortable. You can't feel comfortable when you turn yourself out there with animals, you can't escape human civilization, you can't escape man's progress, embrace man's progress because man's progress is really your progress.

Whatever man is able to achieve it's proof that G-d made you valuable because you have the same thing that man has. You have a brain, hands to work with, a human soul, you have the same things the achiever has. Whatever the achiever has you have it, you might say "But I have been held back." Don't you think the first man was held back? You go out there plant and build a house, a storm comes through and knocks his little cheap house down, wash out all of his works. He goes out in the morning and there is nothing there and he worked all of his life for it, did he give up? No he didn't even though he might be old and too weak to work. His children and the young folks related to him and his friends, they get busy and pretty soon they put another house up, are we prepare to do that? We let something wash us out, knock us down and set us back and we're finished and we're on welfare eternally, no spirit to change, wake up.

Some of us, we want the life that respects the value that G-d gave us and put in us, we want a life that respects that value. I don't want a life where I don't have to use my brain. Muhammad the Prophet (pbuh) said, "There is no greater thing that G-d has made than the human brain." And when we look at the works of the human brain we know the heart makes a contribution, it gets the brain started and makes requisitions to the brain. The heart says, "That is a beautiful house there but it is a little bit rough or it doesn't have enough flowers and plants, put some trees around it," this is the heart speaking. The brain listens to the heart and says "That makes sense." Then the brains sets out to achieve it, and makes that beautiful house that your heart wants, making it beautiful and comfortable like your heart wants it, but what did the work? Was it the heart or the brain? The heart makes the requisition, the brain does the work. You have to respect your brain and know it is above the brains of all other living things. You are favored with your brains to do things that they cannot do.

Don't you know a roach still lives like a roach lived three thousand years ago in the palace of Pharaoh, I know because I read about the history of the Pharaohs, they have pictures they carved in stone of roaches. I don't know why. If these roaches don't stop bothering us in our apartment one day some of us are going to have a religion and we're going to put some roaches up in stone saying, "These are some durable creature, these everlasting creatures." We might give them a place in the heavens.

I'm making humor, but I'm not carrying on for fun I'm very, very serious. The roach, the way he lived three thousand years ago in the palace of the Pharaoh is the same way he lives right now in your palace. The same way he crawls around, when you turn the light on he runs and hides, you turn the light off he is back out there trying to find the sugar or whatever you dropped off the table, maybe a half of a pork chop or chicken.

Man Was Created Upon Life, Human Nature

You do not have any money but you work the garbage collectors more than any other people. The rich don't work the garbage collectors like our poor folks in our neighborhoods.

There is something bringing out those roaches and the rats, but they don't have any history to show that their advanced. They are still living on the same low level of nature that they were created upon.

Man was created upon life, human nature, but he was also created upon animal nature and he rose up out of the animal nature, he woke up to his own value and he saw himself higher than the apes and other animals, monkeys, dogs and he prided himself and said, "I'm human," meaning I'm not meant to act like a dog, I'm not meant to be a wolf or something, I'm meant to be human. I'm not meant to be a buzzard not even an eagle. I'm better than that." And man proved in time that he is better than all of the animals and everything they can do. Man watched the ducks fly and land in the water and some can go down deep swimming in the water like a fish and then come up to the surface and ride the surface and later take off and fly in the air. Man finally caught up with it and said, "I have more on you than language, freedom of movement I'm going to show you something." Man made a vehicle that can go down in the water, come up, take off from the water it does what the duck can do. Whatever man saw anything else doing, eventually he was able to do it.

The eagles flies above the storm. Man says, "I'm not going to be satisfied until I make an airplane to fly above the storm." Now we have airplanes that fly above the storms looking down on the clouds and lightening flashing, that is man and that is what everyone of you are, you are human. Wake up to your value and stop disrespecting the great value that G-d made you. If you have a friend or a child and you give them a precious thing as a gift for its birthday or whatever the occasion, if you see they don't care about it leaving it on the floor with the trash it hurts you.

I know G-d does not hurt like we hurt. He is protected from this vulnerability or these weaknesses that we have, but you should at least imagine that whether G-d experiences hurt or sadness or not how do you think G-d is by you when He sees you take the most precious thing He gave anything in the world? He never gave any living thing or anything dead the value that He gave you. Then He catches you putting your body in the garbage can. That is what you're doing by the corruption that you let come into your life. You are putting your body, the gift G-d gave you, your life in the garbage can and asking the government to pull it out.

The garbage truck takes you and your garbage to the dump that is sad, but that is the state of many of us right now. Some of us listening to this live broadcast are in that situation where you are treating your own life as garbage and blaming everybody and everything but your own self. Wake up to the great value that you have as a human being, wake up to the great help that you have for yourself as a human brain, not a freak brain. If you let the Satan's temptations, his vices and whatever, get you into a life of corruption and you like it you have a freak brain not a human brain. You are not happy unless you are bouncing up and down like a yoyo, you have a freak brain in your body controlling you, you have turned your human brain off it is not on for you anymore. Wake up to your human excellence and come back to human life from that hell you have made for yourself following the way of the immoral public, don't go the way of the immoral public, wake up be at the controls yourself.

There is no better friend or helper than the true person that we were born with when we came from our mothers. When we were delivered from our mothers as babies, we were delivered true people. If you go back to that innocence, to that goodness, to that innocent life we call the life of the infant or the baby you will be going back to your true life.

Come Back To Your Human Selves And Appreciate, Value Your Human Life

And if you can get back connected with your true life then you'll have a spirit to build upon the goodness and upon the excellence of life and not live a life of recklessness, insane pleasures, violence, drugs, alcohol. Some people give their life to stupidity and they are looking for a stupid person so they can have some competition. They give their life to stupidity and go outside to see if they can find a stupid person so that they can have some competition saying, "This guy thinks he's nuts let me show him, he hasn't seen a fool until he has seen me." That is what happens when we get separated from our human life, so we have to get it together. Your life is hurting us. Most of us don't care, but there are many of us who do care and as long as there are human beings separated from their human spirit and life suffering corruption, violence, misery, we can't be happy at home or anywhere until we see you come back to your human selves and appreciate, value your human life. Then we can be happy.

We're Economically Dead As A People

We need that if we're going to change the look of African American neighborhoods or black neighborhoods. We know we have individuals who excel making more money than blacks every made since we been here on this continent in this part of the world, but how do you think they feel when they go home and turn on the television and get the reports of the black neighborhoods? When they hear or see the state of the African American or the black neighborhoods, how do you think they feel, how do you think Oprah Winfrey feels when she becomes conscious of the neighborhoods of

African American people? How everybody but a black man can make business in a black neighborhood, how do you think she feels? She has to feel bad. So none of us can really be happy and free from the misery of all of us until at least we look like and resemble people who have a conscience. We don't resemble people who have a conscience.

Spanish people are conscience, they are conscious of being Spanish, conscious of respecting their own family, the Spanish people's life, they have a pride in work. We know a lot of them are violent too, the big evils of the city are just too much for many people but still their achievements are better than ours when we look at the community life. I can go into a Spanish neighborhood and ride down the streets for blocks and see nothing but Spanish stores, Spanish businesses advertised.

I come back home to my neighborhood., we're economically dead as a people. I did not say commercially dead, you are commercially alive, you spend some money, but you're economically dead. Economics is the science of how money works and how those things that represent money work, material goods, etc. Economics is the study of that. It has to do with the material life of society and how it is converted to money and how money is a medium of exchange for us to buy these material things and live in these material quarters.

Since we are not having business producing wealth, we are economically dead. We may be dollar-wise alive, we may be business-wise alive. You dress up in your business suit go and work for somebody's business, most likely it is out of your neighborhood and you come back to your neighborhood but you don't have any business in your neighborhood. So in business you're alive, money-wise you're alive but economically you're dead.

When you read of great religion how they speak of multiplying and everything, great love for family, increasing in children, the joy of a man, in more sons and daughters, the joy of the mother in more children until the blacks are freed from slavery and then the joy is no more having big families. We have everybody wanting to cut down on the number of children, we have changed everybody, some say, "If I have too many children I'm going to have too many headaches. I have another child who is going to go to public school, I can't afford a private school, a public school is just what it says a school with the public in it. I don't want my children going to that school. I know we planned to have 25 children like grand mama and grandpa had down in Georgia but let's make it one digit not 25 how about two? I think maybe we can manage two. " Sometimes two will give them so much hell they wish they did not have any.

Times have changed not because plenty is not here, we have more than we ever had, times have changed because the mind has changed from being religious and human to being public crazy.

And with that I want to conclude this part of the address, it is a live broadcast and we're happy to be speaking to you and we hope that you will tune in every first Sunday in fact I wish I could talk to you everyday it might happen one day. Our friends in the human family in the radio listening audience we appreciate you being with us and we hope to see you next first Sunday February for this live broadcast. We want to thank our sponsors, the radio stations for welcoming us and we wish all of you a beautiful, prosperous, blessed new year peace be on you As Salaam Alaikum.

G-d is greater, Allahu Akbar, we're coming from the live broadcast to the beautiful environment here looking at you. You are very beautiful, you look like you have your human spirit inside of those bodies, you have not been separated from your human spirit, praise be to Allah (swt). Thank G-d for our life and our presence, that we are still in the state of the original man.

The man that G-d made to be human and he was human. G-d made him human and he was able to keep his human form and life and start the generation of life for human beings and families all around the world, I'm talking about Adam, the one who is a concept in our religion representing the human type that the Creator made, the original man, the first man, the first human.

We were taught that we are the original man in the time before my leadership. We were taught to respect each other, appreciate each other and be happy to be with each other and make sacrifices for the benefit of the whole of our people unselfishly, for the good of the whole of our people. That is where we have to be now and that is where we have to stay. I don't know why people think more of words than they do of life. It wasn't any pain for me to make the steps that I made to come to agreement with Quran, the Book that we were claiming, to come to agreement with the Prophet (pbuh) of that Quran the one who received that Quran, Muhammad the Messenger of G-d (pbuh). It was no big deal for me to conform to that, in fact it was a relief for me to conform to that. My human nature, my human soul just wouldn't let me be knowing with my mind and my knowledge that we were not in accord with that, it made me uncomfortable. The more I got with that, the more comfortable I got in my soul and in my mind.

I had plenty of help for me to do that from my father. He told me to think and be intelligent. He told me to think deep and not to take things on the surface without digging deep to see what is under it. He trained me to dig and see what is under the cover of the language in the book.

And when I obeyed him, I started pulling out stuff that said, "This Temple has to be torn down in three days so we can raise it up again." I said, "The Temple wasn't put here to stay, it was built to be torn down in three days so a new one would be erected." Praise be to Allah (swt) and that is what we set out to do under my leadership, thank G-d and we accomplished it, but still I look at you and you look like you're still waiting, it looks like it is February 1975, I think it was about 5 o'clock when I would speak. You look like you're still right there at that time like I'm greeting you on the first day. Your faces look the same way, I'm not speaking of all of you, but too many in this audience right now, your faces look just like they did on that first day, like you have no idea whatsoever of where we are and where we're going.

Let me tell you where we are, we are forty years from slavery in Egypt and all the old heads that couldn't get new ideas in them are dead and Joshua is saying, "Let us move on," that is where we are. And Joshua is saying, "Don't forget why we are here, we chose not to stay slaves under Pharaoh. We are here to build a new world of our own." We are not here to ask for another master. We did not have an easy time leaving Pharaoh, he killed a lot of us, he tried to kill all of us. That white supremacist, Pharaoh, but we escaped him with the help of good people and G-d's angels now we're in a new land out here in the desert. There is no welfare department to go to. If it is you should imagine, force yourself to say, "No to welfare." Welfare resembles the plantation life only it is worse because the plantation life kept busy my man nature going out working and using my man adult muscles, it kept me getting up in the morning going out working the fields coming back in tired but I was strong. I could lift 150 pound or more, I was strong, now the pimp can't lift anything.

Actually the situation now is worse than plantation, at least we respected somebody who said, "Ok get up go to the field let us do a day's work," but now we have nothing, we're bored to death saying, "Man let me smoke a joint I'm bored to death." After a while the joint isn't strong enough.

After a while he is not even human, he looks like a stone in his face or looks like an old tree with no leaves, like bark as my brother says. He said "Wallace you should have seen so and so he really messed up his life he looks like a dead tree walking." Just wasting our life, we have to change all of this and we're going to change it by doing what I have been speaking on. That is seeing ourselves as not individual life, but community life. Every person has to see himself as community life.

The great wisdom in the scriptures that you read and you don't understand them, things that Jesus said to get his people to see what is the real life, others said it in the Old Testament. David's men said to David, "King you are flesh of our flesh and bone of our bone," they were telling the king you can depend on cooperation because whatever you are here to serve we are here to serve the same and we're going to serve it as though we're one person. You can depend on us to conduct our life in accord with your own personal life. If you can trust your hand you can trust our hand, if you can trust your feet you can trust our feet because we are telling you king we are one body. We are bone of your bone and flesh of your flesh.

Then Jesus comes in the New Testament and tells his following, "You are members of my own body." And if we understand Al Islam it requires of us the same. It says your life and your death is as one single person. If one person can live all the rest can live by following that way of that person. But if we follow one who is corrupt, stupid or insane in his behavior and his life then he takes all of us to death who follow him. So we live in one and we die in one and if there is any single one of us whether it is a Prophet, a saint, a wise man or a teacher male or female who is able to rise up in the life that G-d created for us to draw others to us so they will have the light too, it is only because we have risen up in the human nature that G-d created us for.

Jesus Christ was able to say that because he was in the perfect human nature that G-d created us for. David was able to say that before Jesus Christ because he was in the perfect human nature that G-d created us for. Muhammad (pbuh) is given to us and G-d says of him, "You will certainly find in him an excellent model of life for any who believe in G-d and the hereafter. G-d gives him to us as the model life to emulate, become like that life, live like that, this is the human type, this is the human life, don't behave like those out there destroying, corrupting the neighborhood, making misery for families, don't follow these crazy people find the one who is established on the human pattern that G-d, the Creator, the Designer of the stars in the sky and whatever in the earth, follow that person.

I'm sure we can find more than one, we're not so extinct that there is only Imam W. Deen Mohammed standing up in the human model that G-d wants us in, you can find others but they are very rare.

I heard my father say at the table when they were eating, they called it table talk. Southern people they have table talk, that is just the way of regular folks, to eat and have conversation. It was one of those times my father was talking and he said, "There was a woman and she had a bone and seen in the public walking with the bone in her hand and somebody came up to her and said, 'Woman why are you carrying that bone?' She said, 'It is the bone of a good man.' Good men were so rare, so hard to find that she was holding on to the bone of one who died. You parents raising your children spending all of your money on them, not giving into the corruption of the public life and your daughter is taken by one of these young men and you have to send her money to take care of her and him I know some of you want to go to the graveyard saying "This is where George died let me see if I can find something left," and walk through the downtown area and hope somebody asks you a question, so you can say, "This is the bone of a good man."

G-d wants us to see with our eyes, clearly how we are to know ourselves and the external world. If you could take a lesson from man's world, it could put you back in a situation or in a position to appreciate what G-d offers us, and He always offers the best. You look at man's world; everything he has in order for you to benefit from it you have to use your good senses. Man makes shoes, if you want to wear shoes there is a certain way you put them on. You don't cut a hole in the bottom and try to stick your foot in them that way, they have a place there to put your foot, it goes in the top. If it laces up, you lace it up, if it doesn't you buckle it up or you just slip it in and you walk in the shoe. But there is some kind of sense, an amount of good sense that you need to benefit from anything man made.

Like this cap I'm wearing here, it is supposed to worn like that. I can't wear it on my chin it won't work that well it is supposed to be on the top of my head. A car, most of the youngsters want cars even before they get old enough to drive in, everybody wants their own car, but when you get that car you have to use good sense. You have to follow good sense instructions they give to licensed drivers and the manufacturer who made that car, he knows more about that car than you. He knows how to treat that car better than you do. Isn't G-d the Manufacturer of our human bodies and if you believe that, should He know better how to take care of this human body than we do? They give us a manual saying service this car at the next 5,000 miles, do this and get this and that, you have your car Bible there or your automobile Quran and it is going to tell you how many prayers and if you miss too many of these, your value is going to go down. Maybe you will be driving this car but the value is going down because you didn't keep up the service.

When we look at man's world, don't we see sensible instructions and find ourselves conforming to the direction they give us? To live in this man's world you have to follow directions that they give us. Now you want to live in the world of spirit, in the world of G-d, in the world of soul, heaven and whatever but you don't want to follow any direction you don't want to follow the Book that the Maker gave us. The Maker gave the Book to Moses and before him He gave the Book to Abraham, to Jesus Christ, the Gospel, the Good News. And the Maker gave the Book to Muhammad the Prophet (pbuh) and those Books are for us. All that you have in your world is nothing in comparison to

what G-d gave those servants of His. Your world would not be surviving, not even established if it was not for human beings believing, having faith in those great servants of G-d and preserving what they left and building a new world by the blue print left to them from those great servants of G-d, this is what I know to be a fact.

I Have No Spirit To Sleep In The Face Of Work To Do

We would have no democratic republic if it was not for wise men perceiving and seeing the wisdom in scripture and the direction for human society in scripture, that was the only way they came to this great idea we call America or the democratic republic. I can prove that to anybody who has some sense and knowledge. Anybody if you are read, you know history I can show you from scripture and shine the light of scripture on political history, I can shine the light of scripture on industrial history, the history of industrialized nations. I can shine the light of scripture on all of them and I can show anybody with good common sense and prove to you that scripture was before them with the pattern, the blue print of how to establish that life. So you are being cheated out of a valuable life because you are weak for it, that is the only reason why. You eliminate yourselves. Nobody else eliminates you because you follow sleep, you follow death, you follow surrender, so you eliminate yourselves. **I have no spirit to sleep in the face of work to do**, I have no spirit to die with great hope for tomorrow staring me in the face. Wake up people please.

It is time to demystify this world, take the mystery out of it for the common man. He is the only one who carries the burden and he's left in the dark because he can't be trusted with his own life, but that is the way of one disposition of mind under G-d. There are two main dispositions of mind under G-d. One is the disposition that you can't trust the common man with his life so you have to hoodwink him, keep him in the dark. The other position is that he is a valuable creature created to rise up to any challenge, but G-d gave us this life as a test or a trial. It is to test us as a human body, they say the body congregation. There are many people in the congregation but they use the single noun "Body" that is exactly what we're talking about. One single person but in many, one in the many. One living by the pattern that the many buy and therefore the essential function of life is the

same for all of us equally as though it was one function and
not many functions in many individuals.

We're given language and we need to be educated. Religion
if it can't be trusted to the majority of the people, to the
masses of the people and has to be trusted to just the
enlightened person or the person given revelation we will
stay in the condition we're in now. When most of the people
are nonproductive with terrible burden on their souls, Jesus
Christ, peace be on him, said, "You arrest me in the night and
everything I've done it in the light." Then Muhammad
(pbuh) comes along continuing that work G-d says of him,
"We have given it to you in plain language for it to be made
clear and to clear up matters that are confused or in error."
This is the way and great progress was made for the masses
of people in his day and time, how come it is not done in
these days? It was the common person who followed him,
slaves were freed and even before their freedom they were
already insisting upon being called a Muslim or follower of
Muhammad the Prophet (pbuh). We know what happened to
one of the slaves called Bilal because he wouldn't denounce
the religion and his masters tortured him to get him to
denounce the religion. A companion of the Prophet (pbuh)

Abu Bakr came and bought him from his master so he could have the freedom to practice his religion.

Muhammad (pbuh) attracted the masses of the people and there is a saying of his that makes it very clear, what he is all about, "He was offered a path through the mountains to get where he had to go and he was offered a path through the plains, he chose the path through the plains, this is a saying. What does that mean? He was saying I am not of the nature to want to rule over people, I don't want to establish a government to control people and rule them. I refuse to establish a governmental order, my mission is not to guide people in the building of governments, my mission is to guide people in the building of human life, human families, human communities.

Al Islam is the religion of freedom, justice and equality this is what my father told me and the more I learn about it, it must have been an angel, a messenger in some form that brought them that kind of language; a bird or something. A cat once brought me guidance, help from G-d whether you believe it or not and I still practice the wisdom I learned from that cat right now at home, I shared it with members of my family and I shared it with my friends my cat called P2 panther two. It was the child of its mother panther one, both were beautiful black female cats.

It was a short message, look how easy it was I heard it when I was 6 or 7 years old from the ministers of my father, he used to say it regularly in those days 1940's and even the 1950's that Al Islam is freedom, justice and equality, that makes sense. You're telling blacks to leave the church and become Muslims, why should we leave the church and become Muslims? For freedom, justice and equality. Elijah that is reason enough, count me in, why? Because we were in this country denied equal citizenship and that lasted all the way up to the 1960's.

When the Honorable Elijah Muhammad began preaching there was no equal citizenship for us in this country. You might say, "That was in the South." No, that was everywhere, in the South it was more bitter, cruel and bolder, shameless but in the North it was existing also, the same belief. That you were inferior, not human like other folks and you shouldn't be accepted in their society with them to share their society with them. Stay to yourselves.

I remember reading the Chicago Tribune want ads as a boy, my brother Elijah we can tell you that Chicago Tribune had want ads that said whites only, they let you know don't even go and ask for that job. This isn't Mississippi I'm talking about Chicago. We have had blacks lynched in Chicago, why? Because he was in a neighborhood after dark and some whites caught him and asked him what was he doing there. He said he was coming off of work, he worked late. They lynched him in Cicero, brutal killing of this young man. You want to point the blame on the South, no. The blame has to be pointed on the white supremacist system that was ruling everywhere in America. You want to excuse the North, Boston? Who was the president of Boston when they had us on the plantation? It was the same president who was voted for by those people who had us on the plantation, they voted in one president not two. They didn't vote one president in for the plantation South and another one in for the East and the North.

They voted one president in, so that one president was supported by all those white bigots who were mistreating us in the South. He was supported by them, they voted him in

and he was catering to them not changing the system until the time came when the Quakers, Jews and others joined mainly because of Frederick Douglass' determination and his mental skills, his education and his ability to articulate the problem, to speak very clearly and sharply to reach the hearts and minds of whites in Christianity and shame them out of that ugly thing that they were supporting.

That is what happened to change things, it was changed, thank G-d for all of the good supporters we had from Christians and Jews. Thank G-d for a human soul that couldn't accept to be devaluated and put down below its dignity. Frederick Douglass and many like him males and females, thank G-d that they stood up in their human nature, human excellence and demanded their rights.

You look at the world today and you see the laws have changed, thank G-d for that too. We can go to court and get the sentence to punish the people who deny us our rights, we can get that now. But you are waiting for Jesus Christ to come and take you up in his arms and say, "You have no more worries now Mary, I'm here for you. I'll make sure the lights are turned on at night in the house and I'll make sure they are turned off for bedtime and I'll make sure the water bill is paid.

And I will clean up the kitchen for you, I'll make up the bed and get up all of the things you have strewn all over the room. That boy who is on drugs I'll take care of that for you too, that daughter who won't go to school and just want to lay up here in the bed with that pimp of hers, I'll take care of that too for you honey." You are waiting on Jesus Christ, some savior to come in.

G-d says to us in our religion, "You who have faith save your own selves and your families from the fires of passion." Passion for wrong things and not passion for the right things. G-d says save yourselves so don't think you're going to get a Jesus Christ to come to you and take on your burden and do everything for you that G-d made you to do for yourself. Don't hope for that. G-d wants you to see the great edifice that He made when He made you.

Some people care more about looking pretty than being comfortable, a young lady goes out and she has an outfit that she just has to wear and it is 10 above zero. She is out in the

cold weather, the Chicago wind is whipping her and her breast are showing, the body is naked almost like she is wearing a swim suit and she is having a good time Christmas Eve. When New Year comes she is in the bed sick. I care more about life than I care about the way you look at me or the way you feel when you see me. I don't want you to say, "He's handsome," no say he's ugly. I'll put a monster coat over me and look ugly, I don't care if that is what it takes to keep me warm and keep me from getting sick tonight. You don't have to like the way I look, turn your head.

G-d says He has made this world to support our life and to give us all that we need for our life, isn't that wonderful? Observe the sky. G-d says when this world is finished the hereafter that He will give to those who earned it will be the same as the space of the skies and the earth combined. So G-d didn't say in our religion and I don't think He said it in other religions either that when you get to the hereafter you're going up in the sky. He said if you want to go up in the sky go there, but also it is going to be the space down here too.

The hereafter is going to be the space down here and up there, all of it. That is going to be the space for us to occupy, now isn't that good news? That is what Jesus Christ came to give to the world and some of them got it. Some of the favored, saintly leaders they got the right understanding. G-d frees our soul to live in all the space that He, Himself created. Man has gone to the skies and has also occupied the earth.

It says when they get to the new life they will say this resembles what we were in before," do you hear that? This is not me talking, this is what Muhammad the Prophet (pbuh) left for us, from G-d talking. If G-d is going to do justice by me don't give me something looking like E.T. for a wife in heaven, I want somebody looking like Shirley or some of these women who I fell in love with while I was down here on earth. Don't mistreat me and call it heaven. G-d is not going to mistreat us. He said you're going to say this resembles what we had before.

G-d Knows Human Nature And He Wants To Awaken Human Nature In Us

The older I get the more I love water. G-d tells us plainly but how many of us will see, He makes it easy but we make it difficult. You don't need everybody knowing how to get to the new world or the promised land, you only need one knowing. If that one is decent, he is going to share it with everybody else; the signs that G-d wants us to see. Don't expect everybody to see it, that is not the way of G-d, that is not the way of intelligence. The way of intelligence, the way of G-d is to give it to one and the one gives it to others. What is the good in this, is it just economy?

Someone might say, "G-d made it less difficult or less expensive on Him by giving it to just one." No, it is not just economy to make it less of a problem. G-d knows human nature and He wants to awaken human nature in us. He knows if He gives it to the right one, that one is going to share it will all of the others and that is going to awaken in the others that same charity, that same goodness when they see it displayed by one of them. They love that person and they are influenced by his goodness and they become good or better.

This is how Allah (swt) awakens the best that is in us by giving it to one and the one shares it with us and then we love him because of his goodness, his generosity, his unselfishness, we love him for that and that awakens that same thing in us. The same excellence that he has begins to be nourished by his sentiments and by his goodness, it nourishes the ground for that thing to spring up in us and become a great life, this is the way of G-d.

So don't think when I speak all of you should know, thinking, "I'm waiting to see if he's going to say the right thing." Do you know the right thing? Where did you come from? Please let me get acquainted with you, you sure didn't come from the ghetto if you know the right thing because you would have changed that ghetto, you would be doing just what I'm doing.

You would have a business in the ghetto or you would be telling the people to wake up to the absence of business in our name, do something about these neighborhoods, you would be on the case. So don't pretend you know something, be like I am and I got this from the saints before me, we say we know nothing, G-d You know we know nothing,

whatever we know is only because of Your mercy and your love for Your creatures that we know. On our own we know nothing. We come in the world knowing nothing and some of us go out the same way.

Many say, "What is he doing, he is not supposed to be doing this if he is really blessed to see these things he should know he is not supposed to be sharing this with the common people." G-d says in the scriptures, "Observe how the sky is raised up." and He says "Observe the camel." He has humps that go up on its back. The canopy of the sky way above us the distance seem to be immeasurable, we can never imagine where it stops it is so high, so far out of reach.

We see some mountains and I have been at the foot of some mountains and looked at the top and had a little experience climbing so I know it was hopeless for me to want to climb up to the top of that mountain. It will wear you out, defeat you, you would be found dead or just start falling back down. G-d says there are signs in these things, in the creation itself and also signs in you. What is G-d talking about when He tells us how the sky is raised over us? Is G-d telling us just to look up at the sky like a dog or a monkey? They look up at the sky what is it going to do for them? They have been looking at the sky for millions of years the sky hasn't changed their life. G-d says observe the sky, what is He saying to us? Not the sky of that creation, the sky of your own creation, that is what He wants you to observe, but take from the world that I, G-d have made a lesson. Let My world give you a message for the ordering of your world.

See how My sky is raised up so high and beautiful, do you see how peaceful it is? When the clouds roll by they are in the lower region, the blue sky is far out there above clouds. When you look out there on a clear night and you observe My creation, My art work, My design, My order and how quiet it is up there isn't it restful? How peace it is.

When you make your sky pattern your sky after Mine so when your subjects look up at your sky they feel peace, they feel order, they feel the absence of trouble, they see beauty. This is the reason why G-d is telling us about the sky, you don't need a Prophet to tell you to look up at the sky, rats look up at the sky when they go outside but they can't get up there.

For English speaking people the sky is called heaven for Arabic speaking people it is called sky there are no two words for sky in Arabic. If you want to say heaven you still have to say sky. So the little child hears his father, mother or brother saying "One day we will be in the heavens," he is going to hear the word skies. There is no different word, it is the same word for the one, the stars, clouds are in that, is what he's going to hear, one word. When he hears heaven he's going to get a picture of the earth, clear, pure waters, gardens underneath which rivers flow, I don't have to look up to find gardens, to find rivers I look down here. In the Arabic language when you hear the word heavens your mind comes down here (to the earth) and when you hear the word heaven in English you mind goes up there (Clouds). It is true, peace is up there.

What you need for your soul as a condition is sky, what you need for your mortal life as a condition is earth. G-d didn't make us to be spirits without bodies. G-d made a body for a spirit to come into, not a spirit to get rid of a body. And some people, some holy saints think the spirit has to get rid of the body, thinking, "This body is nonexisting and then I can live the spirit."

G-d wants you first in a body and the body invites the spirit. G-d made for your soul the sky, what sky is that? In this world you have more than one sky, you have Hollywood skies, Los Angeles is a place where they make most of their stars. Lost Angeles is lost angels, a sky full of lost angels. If you are lost in Chicago we will give you a job acting and you can go straight to heaven and become one of the stars in heaven. Don't be a lost soul in Chicago you have acting talents, come here and go to heaven. The secular world they feel so bad looking at the religious world preaching and singing heaven all the time and going to hell all of the time so they say, "We are not trying to compete with G-d but we're going to tell them to come here and be stars."

It Is Inevitable That Freedom And Justice Be Established

I want you to know there are seven heavens if you forgot and one of those heavens is the heaven of business accomplishment, of material achievement. One of those heavens is a heaven of the fulfillment of material aspirations.

The Quran says, "See the mountains how they are structured and raised high." That is great material establishment symbolized or pictures as a mountain. Moses went up in the mountain and the Jews came out rich.

Dr. King went up the mountain too, he said, "I have been to the mountain top." But look at the ghetto, look at the neighborhood. What mountain was that? No change over his followers, not economically, they are still described as economic failures, the neighborhood of the blacks or African Americans is one big business failure. So what mountain did our Moses, Dr. Martin Luther King Jr. go up to? The mountain of enlightenment. He was able to see with his intelligence and his education the future for those down here on earth. When you go up on top of a high mountain you look down onto the earth on all of the people all around. It is like being in a plane. Some planes don't fly as high as some mountains are raised up, that is a fact.

He was enlightened to see the future for society on this earth and he was ready to die. He knew they didn't want him around and he knew they were going to kill him, but he was telling us, "I'm ready to die because I know they can't stop it, it is inevitable that freedom and justice be established." That is what he saw. He saw the Hand of Divine Intervention and he also saw the purpose of G-d for the creation of man in society.

He knew that their way was in direct opposition to the will of G-d and the way of nature and that eventually the way of nature in man would work him out of this bad situation. And there would be no more segregation but there would be equality of opportunity for all citizens. He saw that with his wisdom and his insight and he got great help from the Bible to understand it and he was ready to die.

A real Muslim or a real Christian being like Christ nature are ready to die any time G-d calls us and we're happy to go if we know it is G-d Who is calling us. I'm talking about this association that you are in with me. Wouldn't it be beautiful if we could look at them and see the beauty of stars in the heaven? They give us the security of order and not conflict and they communicate to us, impart to us from their stature peace for our souls, wouldn't that be wonderful?

Looking at the sky G-d is saying, "Man hope for a sky of your leaders, of your stars like My sky that I made for you," that is what He is saying. He says, "See how the mountains are raised up high" he raise them up like that so that the earth would not shake with you. What earth?

The earth of material accomplishments. Is you don't want your business to shake and fall, if you don't want your material life to crumble then establish men in the leadership of business solid like a mountain and towering up with material achievements for themselves like a high mountain. Don't follow anybody who had peanut shells all around him and there is nothing higher than his peanut shells. He is eating the peanuts and dropping the shells. Find a man with achievement and model yourself after him and make him your business leader. You see the great wisdom, do you see how G-d is communicating?

Now you rather go and follow somebody who is going to tell you to count the beads and make so many rakats and do this and tell you, "No brother the sky is the sky. What is this that the Imam is telling you, no the sky is sky everybody knows the sky G-d said the sky it means the sky. Did you pay your zakat, the sadaqa Eid, put it in the basket brother? Did you make salat? Here is my rug, make it now." And you make your salat and he is looking for another fool.

He is looking for another fool saying, "Come here brother the Imam Mohammed is wrong the mountain is the mountain, Moses went up a real mountain, this stuff he is talking about you leave that brother you're going back to bidah, back to Elijah Muhammad darkness." If that is the way you're going come to me physically, walk to me then I want you to turn around I want to kick you in your behind and help you go where you want to go. If you want to go to that crap I will give you a boost. G-d knows my soul has never been in this body to accept cheating, I don't want religion or the world cheating me out of what my life is created for. G-d did not create me for that crap and I don't want anybody cheating me out of what my G-d created me for.

If you don't understand it correctly it is working against your productivity, your good life, your good spirit, even your health. Falsehood works against truth, it works against good life. Muhammad the Prophet (pbuh) said the time will come when they will see Christ Jesus and him together. He was

saying right now or in these circumstances or in this time for the

circumstances that man has to accept you can't see us together, you think I'm an adversary or I'm in competition in some kind of effort to pull away from Christ, to take from Christ his following or to hurt the Christian hope, no. He said there is coming a time when you will come to see us together.

I mentioned the Prophet (pbuh) being given the freedom or the right of choice to choose the path to his destiny that takes him through the mountains or the path that takes him through the plains. He said he chose the path that takes him through the plain meaning.

I choose to fulfill my mission with the masses, the common people not with the mountains, the rich, the mighty, the bosses, the rulers, no. This is good but if you take what I'm saying in another way it is bad. If you think I'm saying he went out to topple governments you are wrong and that is a bad perception. He was saying that religion connecting people back with G-d does not depend on material wealth and power, academic knowledge and power, it does not depend on all of these mountains of achievements and power.

It depends on nothing but the common person in his best human spirit and nature responding to the invitation that G-d has given me to give to them. A new life will be bred and from the ground will come up new worlds and a people who will eventually have their mountains, but they will know that the mountains didn't make them, the spirit of G-d and his guidance made them and also made them able to raise up their mountains, this is the way of religion. Was Jesus Christ saying it different? No. that is why he said you will see us together.

Jesus Christ is pictured in the Bible being welcomed into the city and the people threw their palm branches and Easter is coming up soon, in fact I can already smell Easter. This materialist over here he has these holidays so close together as soon as one is gone you start smelling the next one. Thanks Giving, Christmas just stay in the house and eat popcorn and drink coffee, tea whatever Easter will be there soon you don't have but a short wait.

It is okay if we live for G-d and not for the holidays, then they are beautiful, without hangovers, jail terms. More people from the ghetto go to jail than any other time, if jail wasn't so crowded it would be more of them going to jail, but now the police take them out and say, "Go home we don't have anywhere to put you. You didn't do anything but put out the eye of your friend on the dance floor, you stabbed him in the eye, he was blind in both eyes already, go on home. "

Jesus Christ is pictured coming into the city victorious and they threw palm branches down in his path for him to walk on, not a red carpet but a palm leaf carpet. That was their livelihood, palm trees supported them, so they threw what they cherished, valued saying, "You are the man not us, we trust ourselves and our way of life to you."

He rode in on a donkey victorious, the same Bible in the Old Testament has Baal riding a donkey and keeping it in donkey life. Who is the donkey? Everything is a sign, G-d is speaking through signs. Moses was trying to lead his people and they were so busy questioning him and doubting him that they made so much trouble he could have gotten done what he had to do much faster if it wasn't for them just constantly questioning, doubting and making trouble for his leadership. G-d blessed him with a sign to show them that when they saw it, it was a healing for them to take them out of that argumentative state of mind where they would just be disputing all of the time with wisdom and guidance. In the Quran it says, "The ignorant ones say," meaning these are the ones who just contend, always doubting.

The donkey is an unruly animal isn't he? He is given to changes of spirit. He will be cooperating with you, then he'll braw and balk. You talk to him and get back on his back and he'll braw. One man said he got off of the donkey and took a two by four and hit him in the face with it and he got back on him and he rode without trouble for a while. I don't think so the nature of a donkey, you have to kill it. You might say, "If you kill it you will kill your ride too." Donkey represents that type of spirit and mind in people. It can be a white man, red man, yellow man but most of the time it is a Negro.

It is said in the Bible of Jesus Christ that he said to the leaders, the establishment, "Give me your tired and unwanted," your way doesn't bring them happiness or peace and you don't like them, they are not producing anything. They don't contribute hardly anything to your establishment, so why should you carry this burden on yourself? This is a strategy, Jesus Christ is using a strategy guided by G-d. If I go to those people they think they know everything they are not going to listen to me, but if I get the common people they don't think they know everything, they will listen to me. Let me reduce the amount of trouble I can expect from them by appealing to their need to get rid of this burden. That was his strategy.

He didn't go through the mountain either did he? He chose a path through the plains, he reached for the rejected masses, understand back there in that time it was just a few people who were not discriminated against. All females were discriminated against, they thought males were the only ones who had the divine spark and all ignorant people were discriminated against. They didn't have any morals or ethics that demanded of them that they open up schools to educate all of their public, they regarded their public like dumb animals that should be treated like dumb animals. If they don't work beat them, if they get in your way and won't move shot them, hang them, kill them that was the order of that time gone by.

He was appealing not to just the black, some of you say, "I knew Jesus was for the black man, he came in with that donkey into the city victorious that is us you know." Back then the masses of people, the public were all cheated out of education, cheated out of equal treatment like animals, Jesus came to save communities, not governments because the governments were responsible for the communities being left in the situation they were in. He came to offer a strategy and a way of life to the governments that would benefit them down the road so he used a strategy to get them to open a way for him and not persecute or stop him. He said to his disciples, "Go and you will see a donkey untied." Untied means he doesn't have faith in anything, he's not tied to anything. It didn't say find a donkey untied except to one tie that is the tie of matrimony, they didn't even respect matrimony.

Religion Is Sincerity As The Prophet (Pbuh) Said

Aren't we in a time like that right now when the masses don't respect matrimony? They marry for material conveniences and not really to have families. They don't marry to have families they marry to have material conveniences and a play thing, a bedroom to play in. It was a time like that, don't think we're so far from that time. The material world changes, the establishment changes, the common soul of people can go back while the world is going forward. We can regress while the world is progressing because we are really creatures of spirit and when our intelligence doesn't support our life anymore, we can't make sense of things anymore the spirit life starts to rule and when the spirit life rules we follow spirit. The spirit to play, the spirit to play to have material comforts etc., life needs the pattern that G-d created for it and as one of the Imams said from abroad, "It needs that manual that the manufacture gave the Prophets so that we will know how to manage the soul of human beings."

Religion is sincerity as the Prophet (pbuh) said and it obligates the people or the public and their leaders to be sincere by one another. When the Prophet (pbuh) said sincerity is from the people to their leaders and from the leaders to their people. The leaders are supposed to be sincere with their public, their congregations and the public or congregation is supposed to be sincere with their leaders. You are not supposed to be crooked with each other, vote people in and then go back to your homes and as soon as you run into a little difficulty you start saying what they are not going to do.

Saying, "They are not going to let us do that. They have it, they control it, they are going to keep it." That is the negative talk we hear coming from these voters who are hypocrites, they vote somebody in and when you get a little problem at home, you start knocking the establishment, the system and the political leaders you voted in, blaming everything on them, that it isn't going to work because you're too lazy to make it work. You don't have a hope, a dream or an ambition strong enough to lift you up and guide you forward against odds and against problems to overcome, to go over barrier behind barrier. If you have something in your life that you believe in you don't let any wall stop you, you just get to the wall and start thinking how am I going to take this wall down, climb over it, dig under or go through it.

Imam W. Deen Mohammed will not change. G-d has made me the man I am and I will not accept to be any other kind of man and if I see something in your secret language and G-d gives me the spirit to see it. G-d knows if I see it I'm going to share it with my brothers and sisters, with my loved ones, with my friends and my family members and share it with the most distant human being on this planet earth because that is my nature. I will not keep secret something that I know will help a person.

This world has you under falsehood. Don't think anymore of heavenly sky, heaven is wherever G-d wants to give it to you and I think G-d wants to give us heaven right here in Homewood and every other town we're in throughout these United States, He wants to give us heaven. But you have to learn Imam W. Deen Mohammed's way, his strategy for getting the mountain to smile on us as we pass through walking the plains. You have learn my way thank you very much peace, As Salaam Alaikum.

Chapter 5

PROMOTING EXCELLENCE IN THE BEST TRADITIONS OF AFRICAN AMERICAN PEOPLE
KEEPING THE PROMISE

New York, NY
The First Corinthian Baptist Church
September 18, 2004

Praise be to Allah (swt), Lord of all the Worlds. And we thank you for receiving us so warmly and for our presence here. We worship Allah (swt) alone and associate no deities with Him. And we witness that Muhammad (pbuh) to whom the Qur'an was revealed is the Seal of the Prophets and G-d's Mercy to all the worlds, as G-d says in our Holy Book.

Imam Mohammed Idris introduced something very important for us as Muslims in America and living in a country where Christians are in the great majority. That is that it was Christians who first showed Muhammad (pbuh) and his follower's kindness. It was the Christian ruler of what is called Ethiopia, now the land of the Habishi, who accepted an envoy sent to Ethiopia by the Prophet, himself. He said there was a kind ruler there and that they should go there to seek an escape from the persecution in Mecca.

One of them, who was not expected to be the learned one among them, although he knew Islam, spoke. Others among them were thought to be well known for their knowledge of society and things expected of people who would speak to the ruler of the Habishi.

But this common man among them spoke to the ruler and recited to him passages from the Qur'an on Christ Jesus and his mother, Mary, peace be upon them.

When he recited to him the story in Qur'an on the Blessed Mary and her son, Christ Jesus, peace be on them, the ruler said, "What you have said is very similar to what we have." And when the Meccans, who were very angered that Muhammed (pbuh) had some followers who had escaped and gone to the land of the Habishi, of Ethiopia, right away went out to catch up with them.

They couldn't, so they finally arrived at the place of the ruler of the Habishi, himself. And they demanded, saying, "These are our citizens, hand them over to us." They charged them with teaching something different and disturbing the society of the Meccans, who were idol worshippers.

The ruler refused to return them to these Meccans and told them, "I find no fault with them." So we owe Christian society, the Christian world, at least thanks and appreciation for that. And we owe them, I think, our allegiance. We should be their allies in all good works. And I am an ally of all people doing good works.

Whatever We Do As Muslims And In G-D's Name, It Reflects On Our Religion, And It Reflects On Us.

That's the way Muslims are to be, and that is the way Christians are in their excellence. When you will find a Christian in his or her excellence, you forget that they are Christian, when you spend a little time with them. You forget you are talking with a Christian.

You just feel that you are with your own kind, that is if you are in your excellence. Now if you are out of your excellence, it will not be that way. So we thank Allah (swt) for our presence here, and we pray that Allah (swt) guides us all the way in everything that we endeavor to do in His Name or in the religion of Islam. Whatever we do as Muslims and in G-d's Name, it reflects on our religion, and it reflects on us.

People will blame all of us for what some of us do. And people will think that some of us who misrepresent the religion are the image or right way to see all of us. The correct picture of all of us will be hurt. We have to be careful that even in ignorance not to do something that will spoil the image of Islam, of what is really the true Muslim picture, according to Qur'an and according to the life of Muhammed the Prophet (pbuh).

People think that I speak at random or speak from what the Spirit says I should speak, and they are really complimenting me when they say that. They think I am some real special guy from heaven or somewhere.

There was a sister who heard me give a lecture on the Fig Tree and what it says of Jesus Christ in The Gospel, The New Testament. And at the next class, she brought me a bag of real nice figs, the best I had ever seen. I was so happy, and they were looking so good.

She handed them to me, as though she was handing me the Holy Qur'an or something. She is an educator, and she said, "I have observed you, and I think the way you speak is the Fig Tree."

I had preached on the graduation of the soul in the Qur'an, and it is the same in Christianity, I believe. I am a student of the Bible, and I think I am an excellent student of the Bible.

There is a graduation of the soul, and everything that we need in our life, G-d put it in the soul. The soul is like the seed of your whole life. And the soul is the first to register what you need. And then the soul communicates this to the other parts of the body, mainly the brain, the conscious.

So these graduations that the soul wants for us are given in the Qur'an as the Fig, the Olive and Mt. Sinai. I was speaking on this and describing how the fig fruit is so full of seeds, many, many seeds, while the olive only has one seed. That is the main difference between the two.

The fig comes before the olive in our development; the many brings us to recognize the one. This is really logic that you'll find in colleges and universities; you go from generalities to specifics. Even in logic, you go from generalities the many things considered looking for the logic, and you come to the specifics one logic that ties all things together.

It sets the premise for guiding us into what we are looking for. It is the road of logic that takes us to what we are to perceive or arrive at. So I told her it's what is called spontaneity of thought, for the mind trying to perceive or straining to understand, to put things together in a logical fashion, to address what is puzzling you in a particular context.

Then all of a sudden, you get a burst of ideas and so many beautiful things come to your mind; this is the Blessings of G-d. You get all of these beautiful thoughts and you are so happy. You are thankful to Allah (swt) and say, "Thank You, Allah (swt)." The Light comes on and so many wonderful thoughts are coming together.

But you still have not found the one logic that ties everything together. That logic allows you to have rational logic. I explained to the class the first stage of the development described as "Fig." And I said we still have words in English that can explain to us what this is all about.

If you say or use the expression, "That is a figment of your imagination," that tells us that that idea is not lost from the

English language. And I told them, "G-d taught our Father, Adam, the names of all the things." (Qur'an) And then He exposed them to the Angels, putting them where the Angels could observe them.

Then G-d told the Angels, "Tell me your names, if you know." The Angels could not even tell G-d their names. But the man was created to name all things; that was Adam, our First Father, the developer. Allah (swt) made him of the land and put him on the land, so he would product from the land and develop the land. That is the man that G-d says He taught all the names.

When the Mind is spiritually searching, you are motivated and moved by the soul and spirit to search. That is the Fig Tree. "When you trust faith and trust truth and trust righteousness and believe that there is a G-d Who will reward you for trusting in that way, and you strain to understand, G-d will cause an ignition, something to ignite, to have a starburst, spontaneity, a burst of so many beautiful thoughts and ideas. And you know you have been blessed by G-d. Muhammad (pbuh) says, "That is a step in the excellence of man's life as a rational being." He can't understand some things with his rational mind that are very complicated and too much for his rational mind. But if he strains and has good intentions or purity of intentions, G-d will eventually reward him.

I am not here to teach Christianity. But how can I ignore the Bible, when Allah (swt), our G-d, tells us that this Prophet of ours Muhammad (pbuh) is mentioned in the Torah and in the Injil, that is in the , Old Testament and in the New Testament?

G-d goes on to give a description of this Prophet. He says, "He is one coming to take all the yokes of bondage off of the people and to purify them." G-d says our Prophet is in the Bible, so He has already directed me to go to the Bible, when He said that.

G-d didn't say, "He is in the Bible, but don't look in there." To tell me that Prophet Muhammad (pbuh) is in the Bible, G-d knows, it is telling me to go and see what He is talking about. And I did that and found the exact language in the Bible that is in the Qur'an on Muhammed the Prophet (pbuh).

Then G-d says also speaking of the Qur'an, "In the Qur'an are the Books that were revealed before in their corrected form." So G-d is telling me that our Qur'an contains Books that were given to Jesus, Moses and Abraham.

So we are really misguided, maybe intentionally, by the Satan. Maybe it is Satan's intent to misguide us, in order to turn us against Christians and the Bible. Then it could be our ignorant leaders in our history who left the purity of Muhammad (pbuh).

They are envious and afraid that the Christian world may convert some of us, so they don't have the faith that is strong like Muhammad's (pbuh) faith and the faith of his early followers. They don't have that strong faith. They wouldn't send you to Ethiopia.

The home of my soul is with you folk. I love you so much. And this is not something that happened over night. It happened over a long period of my life. And as an old man, I am getting to see it in full bloom. And it is wonderful.

There are those who fear that if we read the Bible, we will be converted to Christianity and leave Islam alone. There are many who fear that. But if you have something that can't stand the test, don't sell it to me. I don't want to buy it. If it can't stand the test, I don't want it.

I am afraid that if we don't get our hearts back to where they were when we were sincere and innocent following the best of our African American leaders, Frederick Douglass and others, and all of the good religious leaders, for back then we were sincere. We had good intentions and loved our leaders for their courage and their moral strength.

Those leaders had the courage to give us what was best for us. We didn't want leaders who would permit us to do just anything and everything. Or when we were wrong, they would look over our mistakes, just to keep us as friends and followers. We didn't want leaders like that.

We wanted leaders who were true leaders, who were true brothers and sisters and would tell us when something was wrong with us, that would stand in the way of our good life and our progress in the world. That was the kind of leader we wanted, and we had them.

But something happened in the early 1960s. A new leadership came. They misunderstood the Honorable. Elijah Muhammad and thought it was all about Black and Power, being superior as Blacks and having money and power. They went after the things of this world and lost their own souls, as the Scriptures say.

Now after that has happened, we find our people with leaders who are not really having the spirit and the moral strength that the old leaders had. They are great orators and great speakers, but they don't have "something" that those old leaders had.

So they are not reaching too many of us deep in us, who are hungry for help. That life for us didn't start with the Honorable Elijah Muhammad. That life for us didn't start with his teacher, Mr. Fard. They were great people, but that life didn't start with them. That life started even before Frederick Douglass. That life started with the first slave who started asking questions and didn't get answers.

"Why am I a human being like him, but he owns me? But he goes where he wants to, to see his relatives and to marry whom he wants to marry. But I cannot. I'm his property like his horse or like his cow or like his dog or like his mule or like his chicken. I am just his property.

"Why is this? I can't ask him, because he might whip me. There is a G-d somewhere. I see the master praying and talking about G-d. And if You are really G-d, answer me, please. Why have You assigned him to that life and me to this one? And we both seem, in my eyes, to be the same life?"

Questions like that, the slave would ask, just like Muhammad (pbuh) would, looking at the miserable way of his people in the time of ignorance. And he was carrying the burden of his people on his heart.

He would go away from his people and the traffic and their conversations and everyday routine life up into the Mountain of the Light. It is called that because he went up into that

mountain and received The Light. It was not called that
before the Prophet (pbuh) went up there.

Muhammad (pbuh) went up there with the burden of his
people on his heart. He didn't know how to call on G-d. He
wasn't a man of Scripture, but he knew or believed that the
universe was an orderly universe with a definite scheme or
design. That suggested to him, before he ever met G-d, that
there was One Logic tying everything together.

So he went up in the mountain crying to the Higher Heavens
for an understanding. And G-d responded and communicated
to him with five short lines. The Bible says if you knock
long enough, there will be an answer. If you go to the door
and knock, don't give up. Keep knocking. If you are
knocking on the door that G-d has made to open to you, it
will be opened sooner or later. Don't give up.

So those slaves were sincere and were not seeking a small
freedom. I am talking about the real people, not the ones who
were satisfied as an animal would be with what the master
had ordered for him as a life.

Your Life And Your Death Are Like The Death And Life Of One Person.

I am talking about those whose inner core consciousness may have been out of touch with the mind, but nevertheless it is still a consciousness called soul. Those are the ones I am talking about. Those ones did not want for us any small freedom, a freedom from the plow in the field that we plowed or freedom from the immediate space that the master kept us on, so we could go and travel outside of that area and see what was on the other side. Or the freedom to play when we wanted to play.

No, they were seeking a bigger freedom, a freedom to connect themselves with the world that G-d made, the whole heavens and earth, the skies and earth. They wanted the freedom to connect with that and know, "Where am I in this Great Plan? Where am I in this great world that You made, G-d? What should I be doing here?

"Should I be having this small life of a slave? I don't think so, because my soul is not satisfied with this small life! My soul knows better!" That was the kind of thinkers they were. And they are the ones who began to be dissatisfied with their circumstances and have the courage to change it.

Frederick Douglass, we know his story. He was under a slave master who was kind to him and who had a wife who saw great value in Frederick Douglass and wanted him to use his intelligent mind. So she would go and bring him books to read.

But then this good master was pressured financially and saw Frederick Douglass only by the money he would get if he sold him. He didn't want to sell him, he was pressured financially to sell him and sold him to a bad master.

The bad master did not treat Frederick like a human life and treated him like something bought. Soon Frederick Douglass got tired of this treatment and one day in the road, he dropped a sharp right on the jaw of his master, left him there sleeping. And Frederick went on to freedom. Now how come some of you all want to forget Frederick Douglass?

Here is a man who threw one punch and took our life out of slavery, at least in his body. If one succeeds, the whole succeeds, if you understand. G-d says in the Qur'an, "Your life and your death are like the death and life of one person." That was said in the old Scripture also, before the Qur'an.

It only takes one person to lead the whole people into darkness or into ignorance and finally into corruption. One person can lead you into moral and intellectual death. And also one person can save our life or can lead us into life.

That is what it means, that your life and your death is as one person. If one person gets the power and influence, that one person can take the whole people down. Look at what Hitler did to his people. He took the whole of Germany down.

And in Christianity, it is said that one person took us down Adam. It is said Adam fell victim to the suggestions of the devil, Satan, and brought the whole humanity down. Everybody suffered from his fall; because Adam fell, we all fell. And it is true, if you understand it.

What Adam represents is in all of us. Since it fell in him, it means it fell in all of us. And the world came under and influence that killed it in all of us, not in just one physical man or mortal person. It represents one physical type that G-d wanted to be for all of us.

When the world of Satan brought that down, it was brought down in all of us. So all of us died the death of that fall. And one becoming alive in that is the resurrection of all of us. Jesus Christ is the Second Adam, and in him all people can live. But for us Muslims, it is put a little differently, and we don't see that type the first Adam and second Adam as two different types. They are the same type.

Whereas people of the Bible see Adam as one type and Christ as another type, we Muslims see it as that life or human type in its original state that G-d put it in. That is Adam.

But it had not dawn into the conscious of man yet; he had not become educated as to what is this type, what is this life, what is its nature. He could not describe it; he was just living it naturally.

It was his protection, until Satan suggested something to him that was too big for his rational mind. His rational mind couldn't handle it, so he fell victim to the suggestion of Satan and he went astray from that original type.

Now Jesus comes and he is conscious of it. It is not just a nature saving his life. He has a nature, and he is conscious of that nature. He is knowledgeable of that nature. Christians call that the Second Adam.

We don't call it the Second Adam but the same Adam in progression. He is developing life. The type is developing. And the type goes up from Adam, according to the description that Muhammed the Prophet (pbuh) gave us in his ascension or his night visit or travel.

It went from Adam to John the Baptist and Jesus Christ. And it went to Yusuf or Joseph to Ezekiel or we call him Idris. It went up from that level; it was the human life developing, going up into its full picture and scheme and plan for its life that G-d created it for.

It goes up to Prophet Aaron and up to Moses and finally up to Prophet Abraham or Ibrahim. It was seven levels, and every one is a progression of Adam's life. That is why he is called "Father."

Every one of those came out of Adam's life; they were in his picture. And his picture released what had to be released to fulfill the picture that G-d wanted for man Adam and all people.

How do we know that? G-d said there are seven above you and seven within yourselves. It means that whatever was revealed to us or shown to us by Muhammad (pbuh) of what is the elevation are also in us by Muhammad (pbuh) of what is in the elevation are also in us.

Do you think Christians are missing this knowledge? If they were missing it, then why do they speak of a seventh son? And there are seven sons and the seventh son is the one who is blessed the most.

We are told that Abraham was in the highest heaven, the seventh heaven. But we are also told that all of those levels are excellent. And G-d said, "Do not discriminate against My servants; do not make distinctions that would discriminate against one of them."

Do not say that since Abraham is in the seventh heaven that he is better than Adam, no. You don't say that. Abraham is not better than Adam; he is just better situated than Adam. And G-d situated him, as He situated Adam. The credit goes to G-d.

For the end that G-d wants on this earth, Abraham is better situated. But don't say that any Prophet is better. No, they all were excellent and equal in their willingness or in their spirit to serve their G-d.

The Ascension or Night Travel of Prophet Muhammed went from Adam to John the Baptist and Jesus Christ (peace be upon them).

We have to get away from this spirit in us to separate ourselves from our Christian brothers and sisters and even separate ourselves from our Black brothers and sisters or African American brothers and sisters, thinking that we are some kind of natural enemies, just fated to be in some kind of competition with them.

That we are not to mix with them or approve of them; that we are to work to overcome them. That we are to work to defeat them and become the leading people over our African American Christians and take the neighborhoods from them. That is not right, and that is not what Allah (swt) wants for us.

Our life as a people will punish us, if we go against our other African American brothers and sisters. Don't you know that no matter what you convert to, before you concerted to that you were belonging to the life of your people. And what makes our life real for us is our common experiences, our shared experiences, especially those experiences that were very, very strong in our lives — whether negative or positive, whether bad or good.

Slavery was a bad circumstance, and we shared that as a people. Slavery had its way of making impressions not only in our minds but also in our souls. Those impressions in our souls give pictures and design to our soul; they make our soul distinguishable or different from the soul of other people.

It is because in the genes that our fore parents gave to us or that we inherited from' were the genes experiencing American fashion slavery — Southern man fashion, plantation land fashion. The Irish, Polish, Jews, Italians, none of these Americans experienced that. We experienced that, and it has put a print, a design on our very souls and we are different.

We are not like Africans. No, we are not. An African who comes over here and did not experience what we experienced for almost three centuries on the plantations in the South and in the North are not like us.

The President of these United States was not just the president of the northern states but for all of the United States. He and his government and the U.S. Congress were turning their heads and not looking at what was happening in the South. It took a rebellion on the part of good people — Whites and others — who knew it was wrong and that it should not be tolerated.

Among them were the Quakers, the Abolitionists, their efforts and the able spokesman they had in Frederick Douglass to bear so much pressure on the country, and the time came. G-d says, "Wait until I come with My Timepiece. You have your timepiece, and you are planning your world for something to happen at 5 o'clock your time. But I have something that I planned, too, and it is going to happen at 5 o'clock My Time."

Almighty G-d let us remain in that situation, until the time came for us to be freed from that, and He had able and sincere persons existing and in place to put pressure upon the heads of government. They did and the matter was resolved, and we were physically freed.

Now we experienced the life of slaves. From the life of slaves, we experienced the life of so-called free people, freed from physical bondage. But that life was still a life of torment. The Klan terrorized us and took all of the courage out of us, so as free people we couldn't dare show muscle to the White man. The Klan did that with their terrorist tactics.

That is exactly what they used — terrorist tactics to put fear in us, so that we would never rise up or try to show manhood or muscle in front of the White man. But that failed, too. You can't kill the original man. You can't hold him down forever. He will rise again....

ABOUT THE AUTHOR

Imam W. Deen Mohammed was unanimously elected as leader of his community after the passing of his father in 1975; the Honorable Elijah Muhammad, founder, leader, and builder of the Nation of Islam.

At a very early age, Imam Mohammed developed a keen scholastic interest in science, psychology and religion. He began his education, from elementary through secondary school, at the University of Islam in Chicago. Further educational pursuits took him to Wilson Junior College, where he concentrated on microbiology and to the Loop Junior College where he studied English, history, and the social sciences. However, his primary education has come

from, and through, his continued pursuit of religion and social truths.

Imam Mohammed's astute leadership, profound social commentary on major issues, piercing scriptural insight into the Bible, Torah and Qur'an, and his unique ability to apply scriptural interpretation to social issues have brought him numerous awards and high honors. He is a man of vision who has performed many historical 'firsts'.

In 1992, he delivered the first invocation in the U.S. senate to be given by a Muslim. In 1993 he gave an Islamic prayer at President William Jefferson Clinton's first inaugural interfaith prayer service, and again in 1997 at President Clinton's second inaugural interfaith prayer service. His strong interest in interfaith dialogue led him to address the Muslim-Jewish conference on March 6, 1995, with leaders of Islam and reform Judaism in Glencoe, IL. In October of 1996, Imam Mohammed met Pope John Paul, II, at the Vatican, at the invitation of Archbishop William Cardinal Keeler and the Focolare Movement. He met with the Pope again, on October 28, 1999, on the "Eve of the New

Millennium" in St. Peter's basilica with many other world-religious leaders.

In 1997, the Focolare Movement presented him with the "Luminosa Award", for promoting interfaith dialogue, peace, and understanding in the U.S.

In 1999, Imam Mohammed served on the advisory panel for Religious Freedom Abroad, formed by Secretary of State Madeline Albright. He assisted in promoting religious freedom in the United States and abroad.

In April, 2005, Imam Mohammed participated in a program that featured, "a conversation with Imam W. Deen Mohammed and Cardinal George of the Catholic Archdiocese."

There are many more accolades, achievements and accomplishments made by Imam W. Deen Mohammed. His honorary Doctorates, Mayoral, and Gubernatorial Proclamations give testament to his recognized voice, and the benefit of his leadership to Muslims and non-Muslims alike. He was appointed to the World Supreme Council of Mosques because of the value of his work and leadership in America.

Today, the dignity and world recognition Imam Mohammed has generated is seen all across the world.

Purchase Copies Of This Publication:

WDM Publications
PO Box 1944, Calumet City, IL 60409

Phone: 708-862-7733
Email: wdmpublications@sbcglobal.net

www.WDMPublications.com

For More On Imam W. Deen Mohammed

The Ministry of Imam W. Deen Mohammed
PO Box 1061, Calumet City, IL 60409

Phone: 708-679-1587
Email: wdmministry@sbcglobal.net

www.TheMosqueCares.com